Deliver Us From Evil

Deliver Us From Evil

Deliverance Ministry Examined

Edited by
Jennifer Strawbridge
Isabelle Hamley
and
Nicholas Adams

Published in 2024 by SCM Press
Editorial office
3rd Floor, Invicta House,
108–114 Golden Lane,
London EC1Y 0TG, UK
www.scmpress.co.uk

SCM Press is an imprint of Hymns Ancient & Modern Ltd
(a registered charity)

Hymns Ancient & Modern® is a registered trademark of
Hymns Ancient & Modern Ltd
13A Hellesdon Park Road, Norwich,
Norfolk NR6 5DR, UK

Scripture quotations are from the New Revised Standard Version Bible:
Anglicized Edition, copyright © 1989, 1995 National Council of the
Churches of Christ in the United States of America. Used by permission.
All rights reserved worldwide.
Those indicated as RSV are from the Revised Standard Version of the
Bible, copyright 1946, 1952 and 1971 by the Division of Christian
Education of the National Council of the Churches of Christ in the USA.
Used by permission. All rights reserved.

British Library Cataloguing in Publication data

A catalogue record for this book is available
from the British Library

978-0-334-06348-3

Typeset by Mary Matthews
Printed and bound by

Contents

Introduction

Jennifer Strawbridge, Isabelle Hamley
and Nicholas Adams

In the Lord's Prayer, Jesus teaches his followers to pray for deliverance from evil (Matt. 6.9–13; Luke 11.2–4). At the same time, in his ministry, Jesus heals and delivers all kinds of people from physical, mental and spiritual afflictions, restoring physical health and mental wellbeing and returning them to full participation in their communities (e.g. Luke 8.26–39). His disciples undertake this ministry as well, taught and encouraged by Jesus (e.g. Mark 6.7–13).

In the New Testament, as across the Graeco-Roman world more generally at this time, suffering of diverse kinds are described as an attack of evil forces, and the casting out of demons or spirits was often a speciality of religious healers. Nevertheless, the ways in which evil and suffering are described, along with stories of deliverance from such evil and suffering, varies across time and cultures. Even the witness of Scripture is not monolithic; there are very few stories outside the Gospels and Acts of demonic possession and exorcism. One common thread, however, is the pattern of believers bringing circumstances around evil and suffering to God in prayer: 'deliver us from evil'. Scripture and Christian traditions offer wide and generous spaces within which evil and suffering can be named and engaged – from the prayers of the psalms and the prophets to Jesus' engagement with those who are suffering – with a trust that God is 'with us' even when we struggle to find words to describe or explain what we or another may be experiencing.

Over time, practice, theology and language have developed so that as with the diversity found in ancient texts, so different communities pray for deliverance in different, though related ways. Increasing understanding of a number of medical conditions is helping Christians identify the causes and presentation of what they may experience as 'evil' through different words, and reaching primarily for medical treatment, though of course this does not preclude prayer. Greater awareness of the ableist language (language that devalues those with disabilities) used within churches and some dominant interpretations of Scripture is also transforming engagement especially with people with disabilities. Some communities readily talk of demons and personalized evil, while others prefer the language of healing and wholeness, and still others may prefer a sharper division between the spiritual and the medical. But in all Christian traditions, Christians pray, bring their concerns to God and, at times, ask others to pray for them. And all recognize the words of the Lord's Prayer taught by Jesus himself, 'deliver us from evil'.

A number of questions drive engagement with evil and suffering, which are in many ways a mystery. Why does a person suffer? Why do bad things happen? How do I understand what is going on in the complex mix of what it means to be human, embodied, and yet with faith that there is more to the world than the physical? The language of evil is language that reaches for words to talk about mystery, to describe things that cannot always be explained or rationalized. Deliverance ministry often takes place within this mysterious space where words fail and faith drives us to the words of Jesus, 'deliver us from evil'.

But this mysterious, and often generous, space is not without boundaries. We may not understand precisely what we are dealing with or praying for, but limits to practices of deliverance are set by theology, pastoral good practice, medical understanding and safeguarding requirements, among others. To pray for deliverance, using the symbols, rituals and prayers that the complex mix of Church and cultural transitions give us is right and appropriate. But it is never appropriate to impose pastoral prayer on someone incapable of consent or unable to express for themselves what they are experiencing. Furthermore, stigmatizing illness – physical or mental – by systematically associating illness with moral evil or demonic possession is not appropriate. The same applies to the use of ableist language to marginalize those with illness or disability as 'other', as not adhering to some assumption of 'normal', and as not having their own voice and agency. The words used in Christian ministry do not simply describe events and what happens to a person, they engage with people with voice and agency and the communities that shape them. When it comes to the ministry of deliverance in particular, we are called to reflect on the reality that communities and individuals are shaped through words and practices and to remember that we engage with mystery within the community of faith.

The chapters that follow in this book are drawn from a much larger discussion of deliverance within the Church of England and within theological, biblical, anthropological and medical studies. Experts from across disciplines shared their expertise as part of a Church of England conference in 2022. As the Church grapples with the varied practices of and assumptions around deliverance ministry, this book intends to offer a theological foundation to such discussion.

What readers will find is that ways of thinking about deliverance and evil today are shaped by Scripture and by their cultural context. The language used for deliverance also varies enormously and deliverance ministry includes but is not confined simply to language of exorcism.

This is not to say that for some, deliverance is equated with language of exorcism, the casting out of demonic possession or evil. Some request deliverance because they feel caught up in a story that needs change, closure, peace, or rest. Other requests for deliverance may come from those who believe deeply in the immediate presence of evil spirits or demonic manifestations. In addition to people, some locations or memories of past events in a particular place may need healing and deliverance ministry can be invaluable in enabling these things to rest and resolve. Whatever the case, each and every situation needs to be approached with care and pastoral sensitivity.

Evil also takes on a number of definitions. For some such evil is institutional such as social injustice, greed, exploitation of other human beings, ableism and all forms of oppression. For others this evil is social such as poverty or war. Personal or spiritual evils may also form part of a definition such as grief, mental ill-health, fear or anxiety, or spiritual dis-ease. All of these, and more, may lead people to describe their experiences as demonic, evil, or as a form of spiritual attack.

In some contemporary cultures, churches and other religions, spirits and demons are an accepted part of the landscape of religious life. Deliverance in various forms is also a routine part of such groupings and some of those who come to the Church of England seeking help may already have this background.

The first section of this book engages with mental health and vulnerabilities, examining aspects of safeguarding, medical and spiritual practice, mental health, popular culture, contemporary practice and professional boundaries. The second section looks at different theologies and cultural understandings of deliverance, including understandings of evil and an anthropologist's engagement with a London Pentecostal community. The final section examines deliverance, evil and the Bible, engaging directly with the Gospels, Jesus' practices, and how Scripture has been used, and mis-used, in the context of deliverance.

A final note for readers is that what follows contains discussions of sexual trauma, suicide and mental health disability.

PART 1

Mental Health and Vulnerabilities

1

Hearing Demonic Voices

Christopher C. H. Cook

The Christian concept of deliverance covers a broad range of prayers and practices offered in response to a wide spectrum of different experiences and phenomena.[1] Surprisingly little empirical research appears to have been conducted on all of this, but a theologically and scientifically significant phenomenon within this spectrum is the hearing of voices perceived as evil. Hearing evil – or demonic – voices is by no means the only sign taken to indicate the need for deliverance, nor is it a necessary one. Nor, I must emphasize at the outset, does it necessarily imply that deliverance ministry is indicated. Indeed, if anything, in this chapter I will reach the opposite conclusion. Despite these qualifications, I think it provides a helpful focus to inform thinking about the wider ways in which various phenomena taken to be signs of the need for deliverance may be differently understood within diverse disciplines, communities and historical periods. An interdisciplinary approach is therefore required.

Voices, in the present context, may be understood as voices heard in the absence of an objectively visible speaker. In scientific terminology, these are auditory verbal hallucinations, a term that is understood by some to be prejudicial but that in fact imposes no particular interpretation upon the meaning or significance of the phenomenon. If someone, let us call her Sarah, says she heard God talking to her, we may refer to this as an auditory verbal hallucination (AVH) without prejudice to whether or not we believe that God may actually have spoken to her in this way. We might thus seek to distinguish between the phenomenology of the experience and its interpretation, although for Sarah herself the two may in fact be inextricably interconnected.

AVHs have traditionally been understood as signs of psychiatric disorders, but we now know that they occur widely in the general population in the absence of mental illness. They may also be associated with religious experience, and especially with experiences in prayer. Accounts of voices that sound like AVHs are found widely in Judeo-Christian Scripture and in the Christian tradition. (For further discussion, see Cook 2018).

In psychiatric phenomenology a sharp distinction used to be made between voices heard out loud in external space and those that were more thought like, heard in inner or subjective space. However, recent research suggests that there is more of a spectrum, with some voices being more in thought, some more out loud, and some being a mix of the two. It is also now clear that voices are not just voices; they have social agency, character and personality. People who hear voices find themselves in dialogue with their voices (as, in fact, most of us do within our own thoughts). Voices may be positive or negative experiences and have differing emotional valence. Demonic voices are typically at the negative end of this spectrum and are often particularly distressing.

With this understanding of voices in place, it is helpful briefly to consider the place of voices, and particularly demonic voices, in Judeo-Christian Scripture, Christian tradition and Christian experience before proceeding to consider their relevance to our understanding of demon possession, deliverance and exorcism.

Scripture

Voices are heard from the first pages of the Bible in Genesis to its closing pages in Revelation.[2] Adam and Eve converse with God in the garden, and also with the serpent.[3] The apocalyptic visions of Revelation include accounts of many voices, as well as perception like experiences in other sensory modalities. The exercise of prophecy, throughout Scripture, is rarely accompanied by a detailed phenomenological description but implicitly involves the hearing of a voice, whether it be more thought like or more out loud. Of course, all of the scriptural accounts of these voices have been subjected to historical-critical scrutiny and have variously been considered according to literal, mythical, literary or other modes of interpretation. Abraham, for example, may or may not have been a literal historical figure who experienced an auditory verbal hallucination. However, for the ordinary reader of Christian Scripture, Abraham nonetheless provides a role model of a man of faith seeking to hear what God has said and be obedient. The Genesis narratives thus set up an expectation, or at least offer the possibility, that men and women might hear the voice of God today in a similar way.

Even if we include the voice of the serpent in Genesis, or the voice of Satan in the book of Job, evil voices are far less common in Scripture than are those that are good, notably the voice of God, but also angelic voices. Turning to the New Testament, voices are heard at key points in the Gospel narratives, such as at the baptism of Jesus, the transfiguration and the resurrection. The nature of these voices remains open to speculation and, a century or more ago, some psychiatrists took them as evidence that Jesus was in fact suffering from a major mental illness. Albert Schweitzer (1948), in his classic rebuttal, *The Psychiatric Study of Jesus*, showed that such arguments were neither an exercise of good psychiatric wisdom nor did they show critical attention to the biblical texts. However, since then, the significance of these voices for Christian spirituality and theology has not been given as much positive attention as it might deserve.

In two of the Gospels, Matthew and Luke, Jesus goes into the desert after his baptism and hears the voice of the devil.[4] This voice echoes, questions and twists the words of the divine voice that Jesus heard just before at his baptism. Where the heavenly baptismal voice said: 'You are my Son ...' the demonic voice introduces a conjunction, turning this into a conditional clause: 'If you are the Son of God ...' The exchange is reminiscent of the voice of the serpent in Eden: 'Did God say ...?' The evil voice thus undermines the divine voice through a dialogue that introduces doubt and questions theocentric interpretation.

Perhaps the most significant consideration here, however, is simply that the central figure in the New Testament who hears a demonic voice is Jesus.[5] The Matthean and Lukan temptation narratives are not included in their respective Gospels as a sign that Jesus is possessed (although the religious authorities will allege that he is) but rather to emphasize that, just as the baptismal voice asserted, he *is* beloved of God, and is thus an adversary of the devil. Whatever our approach to interpretation of the text – as literal history, myth, or narrative device – these texts do not support a view that hearing demonic voices is evidence of demon possession. Neither do the ensuing exorcism narratives, in which Jesus casts evil spirits out of various people, give any indication that those who were possessed were hearing voices. The demons that speak do so through the mouths of those whom they possess. Their voices thus become public voices, uttered by an objectively present speaker. Demonic voices are not encountered in the Gospels in the form of auditory verbal hallucinations.

Christian tradition

There are many figures, throughout Christian history, who are recorded as having heard the voice of God, or else the voices of saints or angels.[6] These accounts cross historical, geographical and theological boundaries, including such figures as Antony of Egypt, Symeon the New Theologian, Hildegaard of Bingen, Francis and Clare of Assisi, Julian of Norwich, Joan of Arc, Teresa of Avila, John Bunyan, William Blake, Florence Nightingale, Teresa of Calcutta, Martin Luther King and many,

many others. Some of these figures, albeit by no means all, also heard demonic voices.

According to Athanasius' *Life of Antony*, Antony of Egypt (*c.* 251–356), following an extended period of conflict with the devil, heard the devil say:

> I tricked many, and I vanquished many, but just now, waging my attack on you and your labours, as I have upon many others, I was too weak. (1980, p. 5)

Paradoxically, but with echoes of the temptation narratives in Matthew and Luke, Athanasius thus uses the demonic voice within his narrative to demonstrate the sanctity of Antony. Antony is a Christ-like figure because he has done battle with Satan and overcome him. The hearing of demonic voices forms a part of the noise of battle. It demarcates more clearly the side that Antony has taken against the forces of evil.

The story of St Antony was to become so well known as to provide a model or template for later emulation. Thus, to take one lesser-known example, Maria Maddalena de' Pazzi (1566–1607), a Carmelite nun, when observed by her sisters to be shaking intensely during one of her mystical experiences, was thought by them to be being beaten by the devil, just as St Antony had been. In fact, she said later that she was not being beaten but was hearing voices swearing. This was taken as evidence not that she was possessed, but rather that she was beloved of God:

> And we think that the Lord let her experience this to purge her because that night he wanted to give her the great present of his wedding ring in order to marry her, as he had done to St. Catherine of Siena. (Maggi and Matter 2000, p. 127).

Demonic voices thus function, within these narratives, to demonstrate the holiness of those who hear them.

Christian experience

There has been less empirical research on demonic voices than one might imagine, and certainly much more scientific research is needed. In one comparison study (Cottam et al. 2011) of people who had heard voices, 3 out of 20 mentally healthy Christians (16%) had heard the voice of the devil, as compared with 6 out of 15 Christians (40%) suffering from a psychotic illness.

Sylvia Mohr and her colleagues (2011) relate the account of a 34-year-old man with a diagnosis of paranoid schizophrenia:

> As a child, I was sexually abused. God gave me the strength to forgive and restored my dignity to me. I hope God will heal me. God gives me the security I need. I pray to be relieved of sadness, the desire to die and anxiety. I still hear voices, but I don't mind any more. They are evil spirits who want to bring me down. I focus on God and I don't listen to them.

The history of childhood sexual abuse is significant and is known to provide an increased risk of hearing voices later in life (Cook 2018, pp. 185–6). In some churches and denominations, the expectation of encounters with the demonic is higher than in others. In a study of 33 members of a US Vineyard church, Cassaniti and Luhrmann (2014) received a 70% positive response to a question about whether or not the respondent had ever felt 'in [their] body' that there was a demonic presence near at hand. We are not told in this study whether or not these subjects also heard demonic voices, but sense of presence (Alderson-Day 2016) and bodily sensations (Woods et al. 2015) seem to be closely related to voice hearing.

In my own collection of 36 first-person Christian accounts of spiritually significant voices (Cook 2020), entitled *Christians Hearing Voices*, seven included some kind of experience with evil voices. In a more systematic and overlapping survey of 58 people who had heard spiritually significant voices only two had heard demonic voices (Cook et al. 2022). This, largely Christian, sample provided an interesting comparison with an early secular study by Woods and colleagues (2015) in which 5 out of 24 people who had heard spiritual voices had heard a demonic voice.

Demonic voices are thus not uncommon, they may be associated with mental disorder, but are also experienced by Christians who are mentally healthy.

Possession

The phenomenon of demon possession has been subjected to less empirical research than one might imagine, but it is a topic of interest within the fields of anthropology (Bourguignon 1976), psychology (Stephenson 2014) and psychiatry (Littlewood 2004), as well as theology. Worldwide, in different places, reports of demon possession are both common and culturally sanctioned. There is also evidence, as in the famous case of the nuns of Loudun (Sluhovsky 2002; Stephenson 2014), that possession states may be psychosocially 'contagious' among otherwise mentally healthy individuals. A psychiatric possession syndrome may, however, also be encountered in the course of mental illness. For example, Enoch and Ball (2001) offer the following definition:

> A possession state can be defined as the presence of a belief, delusional or otherwise, held by an individual (and sometimes by others) that their symptoms, experiences and behaviour are under the influence or control of supernatural forces, often of diabolical origin. (p. 224)

On this basis, a belief in possession may or may not be delusional, but the condition of being 'possessed' is defined on the basis of the beliefs of the individual concerned. It is thus self-defined, rather than being something that is defined by others. Depending upon the cultural context, such an individual may seek medical help or religious help.

Most Christian theological reports on possession and exorcism (e.g. Petitpierre 1972) do not specifically refer to demonic voices, either as evidence of possession or otherwise. However, in individual case reports and first-person accounts, demonic voices not infrequently play a part. Thus, for example, the psychiatrist and popular author, Scott Peck (2005) reports on his conversation with Jersey, a 25-year-old woman with an interest in spiritualism:

> The primary focus of our conversation was her experience with a variety of demons speaking to her, both in her dreams and when awake. The names of these demons seemed to keep changing, as if Jersey were making them up on the spot. Only one of them seemed constant – an entity she called the Lord Josiah. (p. 19)

Scott Peck initially assessed Jersey as showing signs of borderline personality disorder but then came to doubt this diagnosis. The ensuing story is complicated and beyond the scope of this short paper, but an exorcism did eventually appear to be effective.

Another example is provided in *Christians Hearing Voices* (Cook 2020, pp. 116–19). This lady, writing about her experiences under the pseudonym of Perpetua, relates that her voices first began during a church service:

> 'The devil is calling you.'
> 'You cannot escape.'

She asked the priest for help who told her that she was possessed and conducted an exorcism in which four spirits were cast out. She then experienced a kind of seizure in which she found herself on the floor. For a while she felt better, but then a week later she again heard the voice of the devil:

> 'You are possessed.'
> 'You cannot hide this.'
> 'You are under control.'
> 'I will make you dangerous.'
> 'You will pay with your life.'

Perpetua has learned to manage her voices through a combination of prescribed medication and psychological coping strategies.

In a study of 15 subjects with DSM-III Multiple Personality Disorder, 14 of whom underwent exorcism (Bowman 1991), nine cited 'dissociative symptoms such as amnesia, destructive behaviours, passive influence experiences and hearing voices' as a reason for their belief that they were possessed. Unfortunately, exorcism was associated with a negative emotional response, increased symptoms of Post-Traumatic Stress Disorder, emergence of new alters, hospitalization of nine subjects, and negative spiritual responses.

Deliverance ministry may include a wide range of different practices, from simple prayers (e.g. the Lord's prayer in its supplication that God 'deliver us from evil'), through to a major exorcism. Exorcism in turn may include a diverse range of practices. At the extreme end of a spectrum, this may include emotionally charged, sometimes violent and even blatantly unethical practices. The exorcism enacted in the case described by Scott Peck (above) was spread over four days, at times highly emotionally charged, and clearly exhausting for all concerned (Peck 2005, pp. 45–64). In her study of patients with multiple personality disorder (above) Elizabeth Bowman reported, among other things, exorcists yelling/shouting, physical shaking and restraint. Four subjects perceived the exorcism as abusive (and it might be considered somewhat surprising that this number was not higher). However, at the other end of the spectrum, deliverance might include relatively brief and simple prayers, which may even make no explicit mention of the demonic.

It thus appears that demonic voices are not infrequently taken as evidence of demon possession, but that exorcism is at least sometimes, if not often, an unhelpful response. Much more research is needed to better understand this phenomenon, but the general rule would seem to be that if someone is hearing demonic voices the best course of action is referral to a mental health professional. Deliverance ministry, or exorcism, may or may not be helpful but has the potential to do more harm than good.

Conclusion

Demonic voices provide an interesting window into just one phenomenological facet of possession, deliverance and exorcism. Much more research is needed both on demonic voices and on other facets of these experiences, such as other hallucinatory modalities, the belief that one is possessed, the criteria that are taken to indicate that another person is possessed, and the variety of practices and beliefs surrounding deliverance and exorcism. This research should be interdisciplinary, with involvement of theology and religious studies as well as the social and health sciences. Longitudinal outcome studies would also be helpful to better inform the safest and most effective practices, medical and ecclesial, supportive of recovery.

References

Athanasius, 1980, *Athanasius: The Life of Anthony and the Letter to Marcellinus*, trans. Robert C. Gregg, Mahwah, NJ: Paulist Press.

Ben Alderson-Day, 2016, 'The Silent Companions', *The Psychologist* 29, 272–75.

Erika Bourguignon, 1976, *Possession*, Prospect Heights, IL: Waveland.

E. S. Bowman, 1991, 'Clinical and Spiritual Effects of Exorcism in Fifteen Patients with Multiple Personality Disorder', *Dissociation* VI, 222–38.

Julia L. Cassaniti and Tanya Marie Luhrmann, 2014, 'The Cultural Kindling of Spiritual Experiences', *Current Anthropology* 55, 333–43.

Christopher C. H. Cook, 2018, *Hearing Voices, Demonic and Divine: Scientific and Theological Perspectives*, London: Routledge.

Christopher C. H. Cook, 2020, *Christians Hearing Voices: Affirming Experience and Finding Meaning*, London: Jessica Kingsley.

Christopher C. H. Cook, Adam Powell, Ben Alderson-Day and Angela Woods, 2022, 'Hearing Spiritually Significant Voices: A Phenomenological Survey and Taxonomy', *BMJ Medical Humanities*, 48, 273–84.

S. Cottam, S. N. Paul, O. J. Doughty, et al., 2011, 'Does Religious Belief Enable Positive Interpretation of Auditory Hallucinations?: A Comparison of Religious Voice Hearers with and without Psychosis', *Cognitive Neuropsychiatry* 16, 403–21.

M. David Enoch and Hadrian N. Ball, 2001, *Uncommon Psychiatric Syndromes*, London: Arnold.

Roland Littlewood, 2004, 'Possession States', *Psychiatry* 3, 8–10.

Armando Maggi and E. Ann Matter (ed. and trans.), 2000, *Maria Maddalena de' Pazzi: Selected Revelations*, Mahwah, NJ: Paulist Press.

S. Mohr, N. Perroud, C. Gillieron, et al., 2011, 'Spirituality and Religiousness as Predictive Factors of Outcome in Schizophrenia and Schizo-Affective Disorders', *Psychiatry Research* 186, 177–82.

Scott M. Peck, 2005, *Glimpses of the Devil: A Psychiatrist's Personal Account of Possession, Exorcism and Redemption*, New York: Free Press.

Dom Robert Petitpierre (ed.), 1972, *Exorcism: The Report of a Commission Convened by the Bishop of Exeter*, London: SPCK.

Albert Schweitzer, 1948, *The Psychiatric Study of Jesus: Exposition and Criticism*, Boston: Beacon.

Moshe Sluhovsky, 2002, 'The Devil in the Convent', *The American Historical Review* 107, 1379–1411.

Craig E. Stephenson, 2014, 'The Possessions at Loudun', *The Psychologist* 27, 132–35.

Angela Woods, Nev Jones, Ben Alderson-Day, et al., 2015, 'Experiences of Hearing Voices: Analysis of a Novel Phenomenological Survey', *Lancet Psychiatry*, 2.4, 323–31.

Notes

1 Deliverance ministry is taken here to be a broader range of practices including, but not confined to, exorcism – see Introduction for further discussion.

2 For a more extended discussion of the place of voices in Judeo-Christian scripture, see Cook 2018, pp. 57–109.

3 I realize that there are important questions here about the genre of literature that these passages of Genesis represent, their proper interpretation, their historicity, and so won, all of which I have discussed elsewhere (Cook 2018, pp. 39–56, 59–60). However, Adam and Eve hear God speaking, and are aware of God's presence, but are not said to have seen God. Within the narrative, and without prejudice to historical critical discussion or theological interpretation, this may be taken as an account of voice hearing.

4 As with the Genesis narratives, important questions are raised here about the nature of the text and its interpretation. While there might be an implication that the voice of the devil is more than just a voice, this is not completely clear from the text. In any case, voice hearing experiences are typically 'more than just a voice'. For further discussion, see Cook 2018, pp. 84–7.

5 It is, of course, the voice of the devil that Jesus is said to hear, according to Matthew and Luke. Without getting into an extended discussion here we might note that there are no biblical accounts of people being possessed by Satan. However, the scribes assert that Jesus 'has Beelzebul' in Mark's Gospel (3.22) and there are those who say that he casts out demons 'by Beelzebul' in Luke's Gospel (11.15). Hearing the voice of the devil is also taken by some, in contemporary practice, as evidence of the need for deliverance (e.g. Cook 2020, pp. 116–19).

6 Again, a more extended account is provided in my book, *Hearing Voices, Demonic and Divine*: Cook 2018, pp. 110–44.

2

Evil and the Supernatural in Popular Culture

Anne Richards

Some snapshots

A teacher walks down the street, headphones on, scrolling through music tracks on her phone. She is a fan of subgenres of heavy metal such as doom, thrash and death metal. She follows bands with vivid names like Venom,[1] Carcass,[2] or Deicide.[3] As she walks, her head fills with songs about hell, evil, Satan, death and demons, with verbs like 'thundering', 'screaming' 'slaughtering', 'blasting' and 'torturing'.[4]

A police officer goes home from work and throws on Netflix to watch *Hellbound*,[5] a phenomenally popular South Korean series about mysterious and terrifying beings that announce a person's death, arrive at the appointed time, incinerate them and drag them to hell.[6]

Some friends form a group to play a survival horror game like *Resident Evil*,[7] *The Evil Within*,[8] or *Silent Hill*,[9] in which hell-worlds or post-apocalyptic scenarios are populated by zombies or monsters intent on devouring or destroying human beings who must blast them to pieces in order to survive as they navigate the dangerous terrain.

Introduction

Popular culture in the developed world, mediated through TV, video games, music, comic books and online forums, is simply *saturated* with material that references death, judgement, heaven, hell, demons, the Devil, angels, heroes, the undead and a continuous battle for human souls. There are crossovers between the franchises; *Resident Evil* for example, has diversified into live action films, plays, novels and comic books. There are even *Resident Evil* themed restaurants.[10]

For perhaps the majority of churchgoers in the UK today, the screaming lyrics of *Death Satan Black Metal* by Krypt, the bringers of death in *Hellbound* and the monsters of *Resident Evil* are simply unknown. Yet from 2020 the pandemic has brought many more people, who ordinarily have no contact with the Christian church, out of their worlds of popular consumption in order to ask questions about what Covid-19 means in terms of judgement, punishment, demonic intent and especially about the nature of evil in relation to the presence of the virus. However, these people do not come unprepared; they already have ideas about what evil 'means' in their heads, and sometimes those ideas are surprising and worrying.

Take, for example, this disclosure (reproduced by permission) of a very personal horror:

> I am terrified of zombies, I mean, really scared of them. I know they don't exist but they scare me anyway and when I look out of my window into the dark of the night, it is a zombie that I expect to see staggering down my garden and heading towards me. I don't know why, but it has been there ever since I can remember.
>
> I think my fear drives me to watch every zombie film out there, read every zombie Survivors Guide book and discuss zombie survival tactics with my friends. On a surface level we are just chatting geeky stuff but I think on a deeper level I am forcing

myself to plan for a world that I hope that I never see but is still a possibility I need to prepare for.

I know zombies don't exist but in the long dark of the night I rush to lock my door anyway.

This presents Christians with a challenge: in the Lord's Prayer Jesus invites us to pray to God to 'deliver us from evil', but how do people understand these words if they are not getting their ideas and context from Christian faith or indeed from any faith? What ritual, prayer, or escape plan covers the zombies that don't exist but come for you in the night, anyway?

Enquiries about evil during the pandemic

A rich seam of information has come in through enquiries about a range of issues during the pandemic. Such enquiries, typically arriving via social media messaging, have come in to the Church of England's central structures seeking reassurance, advice, prayer, opinion, wisdom, or deliverance. Social media enables links, videos and group chats to be easily shared as well as a degree of anonymity. Groups sometimes hide behind individuals who make the initial contact, so it is not always clear who is asking what question. All of the enquiries in one way or another, pose the question: 'how can we be delivered from evil?' Most of them have never heard of, and would never think to ask about, the Church's theological views on evil or about the ministry of deliverance, or indeed are aware of any kind of routine pastoral care; they are just coping on their own without an organized system of belief or any kind of acquired or inherited faith or community. But in the face of existential crisis, they want to ask the Church about matters of 'evil'.

What is interesting about many of the enquiries received between March 2020 and the present, is that they raise issues that are familiar to Christians in terms of the language that is used about them, but what is *meant* by them is something quite different. There is a set of assumptions about the language that does not come from Christian orthodoxy but from discussions about things in popular culture which are part of the enquirers' daily media consumption. These enquirers want to talk about Jesus, the afterlife, death, judgement, heaven, hell, souls, evil, salvation and deliverance. But they also want to talk about the undead, vampires, zombies, demons, soul-ties, spirit attachments, twin flame experiences, Jesus (again), magick and spell-casting and, when their interests, worries or indeed nightmares about these things are probed, their origins are often in their cultural experiences: books, games, TV, music and online surfing. Those things provide a platform for the conversation to go forward. To provide a pastoral response about the nature of evil, you have to watch, listen, or look. Only then can you enter the narrative on the terms of the enquirer. Listening is a primary response and skill.

This can be difficult. One Church of England bishop, for example, was asked by a child about 'Judgement Day'. This was not an eschatological question, but rather about a WWE wrestling event that the child's parents had had on the television. The child and the bishop were at cross purposes. The child, perhaps sensing someone trustworthy and wise, had opened up about something on his mind. But the bishop had no experience of violent wrestling TV extravaganzas.[11]

This is a challenge to the Church, and to pastoral ministry and the ministry of deliverance if it is to engage effectively with what enquirers are asking of Christians and the things they want to talk about. Deliverance ministry tends to be reactive, but what if the principles of deliverance and what we believe about its effectiveness, could be more proactive, more missiological? What does it take to respond well, pastorally, to those who may have problems articulating their sense of oppression or something wrong, the things that make them sleep with the light on, going over their escape plan?

The kinds of enquiries that have come into the national Church structures in the last few years show that ideas about evil and about oppressive phenomena may arise from a number of things, but popular culture creates frameworks for people to fill with their own imaginations and in some cases, they customize these uncritically with their own DIY spirituality and theology. This means that the response has to pick through unfamiliar and sometimes sensationalist claims or experiences with sensitivity, to uncover the core issues that are creating anxiety and unease. These issues can be a straightforward fear of catching or dying from Covid-19, but also might include exam stress, bereavement, isolation, or unlooked-for supernatural or spiritual experiences.

This does not mean that there is a direct transfer from a particular TV series or music to concerns or fears that prompt asking for deliverance, but rather that these form a *sediment* of narratives against which questions and worries may arise, particularly if there is a catalyst like Covid-19 or the experience of lockdown where people might be watching more TV or surfing the internet, cut off from their usual social contacts. The zombies may have been gently festering in a person's mind but have risen up in response to heightened Covid-19 fear and anxiety – an existential threat conceived as monster rather than some kind of abstract evil.

Consequently, pastoral care and its specialized application in the ministry of deliverance has to be aware of those important themes that emerge and to be sensitive to the language and imagery that is generated by popular culture, and also aware of how these are tested, assimilated or discarded as part of a spiritual journey undertaken in the absence of any community or organized system of belief.

The landscape of this is vast and the amount of material available to consumers ever increasing, creating a back catalogue of narrative about death, sin, suffering, evil, as well as judgement, sacrifice and salvation. Beyond the mainstream materials there are other, more arcane fora about violence and revenge such as drill videos,[12] or so-called 'satanic' cosplay and pornography.[13]

In 2010 the General Synod of the Church of England debated violent video games[14] and it was clear then that this was a landscape of bizarre novelty to most Synod members. Spiritual themes run through all kinds of video games, such as the *Assassin's Creed* series.[15] Even children's games sometimes capitalize on the idea of killing to release souls, such as in *MediEvil*.[16] Yet there are many young people especially who become immersed in the survival horror titles referenced above in which the underlying premise is how, with only your own weapons and skills, to be delivered from the onslaught of evil. The definition of evil is simple: bigger, stronger monsters with better weapons than you, whose only desire is to destroy you, either by physically attacking your player-character or by getting inside your head and warping your sense of what is real, or what matters, or how you make choices.[17]

Themes

Enquiries about evil and the supernatural which have come in during the pandemic have shown 12 main themes where questions about the pandemic have been explicitly linked to items in popular culture as the sense-making background for the questions asked. These are described below:

'Is Covid-19 God's judgement on a wicked world?'

People asking questions about judgement or a 'smiting' God talked about death as an agent and particularly as an evil and active seeker of human beings (the Reaper, or the Devil), exerting malevolent power to remove life, whether or not the person is ready for it or deserves it. Against a background of people dying from Covid-19 and the stories of struggle against the virus in the news, enquirers referenced films such as *Final Destination*.[18] You cannot cheat or out-run death if your number is up, even if you try.

'Is the pandemic evidence that Satan has won the 'battle of good and evil'?'

Enquirers talked about ideas of supernatural evil or Satan or some malevolent personality or entity seeking to enter the world and destroy human beings through points of weakness, sin or frailty. Like the person afflicted by zombie fear above, enquirers talked about struggle between rationalizing events in the context of deep fears and things unknown. Some enquirers talked about heavy metal lyrics, but also the narratives of survival horror games and their soundtracks.[19] Some enquirers referenced the monsters in *Silent Hill: The Room* (2004), a game in which severe damage can only be healed by resting in one safe hiding place and lighting 'holy' candles. The hiding place, however, becomes increasingly infested by hauntings that sap the player's health.

'Where do we go when we die if there's no God?'

Many enquirers wanted to talk about an afterlife without God. There are several recent TV series about a supernatural realm, immortality or an afterlife, including *Miracle Workers*[20] and *Forever*.[21]

A large number of enquirers wanted to talk about a TV series, *The Good Place*,[22] which follows four tortured souls getting themselves out of an experimental hell-world by studying moral philosophy, covering not only Aristotle, Locke, Kant and Nietzsche, but also Scanlon, Singer, Parfit, Dancy and Judith Shklar. The premise is that humans (and demons, it turns out) can self-improve after their deaths and reach a nirvana, beyond which, after a long time of bliss, they choose to become nothing and dissolve into the universe. While there is a Judge of the Dead, various accountants and a chief demon – who is a boring individual in a suit, called Sean – there is no God, afterlife is closer to Sartre's *Huis Clos*, (*No Exit*), and salvation is purely on merit. Hell exists but there is no deliverance from evil except what people can manufacture for themselves.

'If I die, will I go to hell?'

Despite a background of anxiety, many enquirers showed a fascination with hell and the fallen angels or demons that may inhabit it. There is a well-established thread of interest and imagination of hell particularly in science fiction and horror genres.[23] *Hellbound* (see above) has generated many contacts, not just about whether the condemned individuals deserve their fate (one of the condemned is a baby) but about the religious order that pronounces on what is happening and capitalizes on it, and whether it has a relation to the Church. Many of the enquirers had also watched the similarly successful South Korean series *Squid Game*, in which similar themes of torment, vulnerability, psychological horror and entrapment were explored.[24]

'There is a presence around me. Is it good or evil?'

Reports of spiritual experiences rose in the latter half of 2020 and many people wanted to talk about supernatural beings, particularly angels or demons. A number of those enquiries interestingly referred to the dialogue between Michael Sheen and David Tennant in *Good Omens*,[25] but even more were intrigued or confused by the Weeping Angels in *Doctor Who* which are murderous entities disguised as angels. Weeping Angels colonized some people's heads like the zombie, above; in the context of Covid-19, an entity that had an innocuous appearance, 'a flu-like virus', could conceal evil and death-dealing, 'a killer virus'.[26]

Reflecting on this, enquirers asked how you could 'know' whether a supernatural experience of comfort or care was genuine or a satanic trap designed to lure them in. In addition, many people asked about guardian angels, as protectors and deliverers and how to contact, access or control such mighty guardians.

'Can you tell this spirit to go away?'

'I see dead people', from the film *The Sixth Sense*,[27] has become a meme reiterated in film, even down to the protagonists in *The Others*,[28] where the haunted ones turn out to be dead themselves and do not know it. TV films and series reiterate a belief in ghosts as lost souls and in ghosts as presenting a distressed, lost or malevolent presence; this also translates into fear of the undead or vampires. People getting in touch to talk about ghosts also referred to the *Harry Potter* series to discuss the sense that a secret otherworld is inhabited by the unrested dead whose backstories and reasons for their lingering become part of the wizards' and witches' education and contribute to Harry Potter's final defeat of the evil Voldemort.[29] There are whole subcultures around vampire culture[30] and paranormal investigation, some of which themselves offer deliverance.[31]

'The zombie represents all of my worries and fears combined'

Another major theme generated from enquirers was that of the undead, or shapeshifters: vampires, skin-walkers,[32] zombies[33] and aliens driving fear of supernatural evil manifest as malevolent beings that otherwise appear ordinary, walking among us or about to reveal themselves. Enquirers talked about post-apocalyptic survivalist series like *The Walking Dead*[34] but also about vampire-romance films like *Twilight*[35] and the seductiveness and lure of an otherworld, or death itself, 'where I don't have to worry any more'. One person talked about embracing the monster in order to know the worst of evil and then emerging on 'the other side' as a metaphor for catching Covid-19.

'It won't stop until we're all gone, will it?'

The Daleks and Cybermen of *Doctor Who* are well-known 'hide behind the sofa' enemies of humankind, but since Covid-19 there have been more enquiries about mainstream films like *Independence Day*,[36] *Aliens*[37] and *Terminator*, which feature incredibly powerful evil entities that will stop at nothing to eradicate their targets: 'That Terminator is out there, it can't be bargained with, it can't be reasoned with, it doesn't feel pity or remorse or fear, and it absolutely will not stop … ever, until you are dead.'[38] The narratives of these films have resurfaced as a background for new concerns about the pandemic, particularly in the context of conspiracy theories that propose the destruction of the human race by shadowy or supernatural powers. In these films, force must be met with force, and the significant story is one of destructive violence and overcoming. Enquirers wanted to know whether the spiritual 'battle' against powerful evil can be won through faith.

'Are we powerless, after all?'

Some enquiries were about the power that abstract evil or evil entities might have. In referencing series like *Battlestar Galactica*,[39] *Star Wars*,[40] *Dune*,[41] *Westworld*[42] and other popular sci-fi, such conversations were about the powerlessness of human beings to save themselves if biological weapons were unleashed (manufactured-Covid-19 conspiracy theories) or if sentient computers decided to capture and kill human beings.[43] In *Battlestar Galactica*, the Cylons are driven by religious belief and the desire to convert human beings by infiltrating their space-ark and becoming identical in appearance.

'Help me. I am trapped in bad love'

An entire theme of enquiries related to deliverance concerned concepts such as soul-tie or twin flame experiences, in which people who believed they had been cemented together for eternity now wanted to be rid of their ex-partner. In some cases these ideas had been adopted uncritically by churches, offering deliverance or 'exorcism' to break the tie. Some people who had gone through this sometimes finished the process by getting a tattoo of a broken heart or a broken infinity symbol.

People who felt that they had not been delivered from this tie to another person sometimes argued that the other person was now a malevolent presence, a demon or some sort of malignity or psychosexual 'cancer' blighting their lives. Further conversation showed that some of these concepts had been driven in the first place by matchmaking or dating programmes on TV (e.g. *Love Island*)[44] or dating services that offer 'eternal' matching, sometimes in the context of ritual.

'How do I find out the truth of what's gone wrong in my life?'

Some enquirers wanted to think about issues of good and evil as a kind of courtroom battle setting out evidence for and against some of the other questions about whether God or Satan is in control of the world or whether our actions merit salvation or not. The background for this was material in popular culture where heaven/hell/angel/demon/afterlife imagery seems to get attached to detective or crime drama. So, it gets bound up with issues of justice and just desserts and uncovering truths – sometimes set in a kind of limbo or purgatory. Some enquirers referenced *The Lovely Bones*,[45] about a murdered person looking back at this world, but others talked about British series like *Ashes to Ashes*,[46] or American series like *Lost*,[47] *Lucifer*,[48] *Constantine*,[49] or *Dexter*.[50]

There was a similar attempt within this theme to 'solve' the issue of deliverance from evil without reference to God. There would be a 'place' to work these things out, to get answers, which could be self-created in order to set the record straight. Jesus, as a sort of policeman or secret agent, might be able to help with this, because of his insight and love for people, but this Jesus was usually a cypher invoked to be useful, but to be put aside when he was no longer needed.

'We need great Christians, great Christians with gleaming eyes and sharp swords'

Many people wanted to talk about superheroes and superpowers as means of defeating evil: the deliverers from evil. Such enquirers felt that some individuals are endowed with powers of protection and desire to save others, and who are specially equipped to battle evil by simply fighting it out. Some of those enquirers got in contact because they had survived Covid-19 and felt they had been spared for some special mission or purpose which they now had to discern.

Superheroes are a popular theme in popular culture, being present in series like *Doctor Who*, and the DC and Marvel universes and their adaptations, such as *Hellboy*.[51] So, sometimes enquirers came with the expectation that deliverance from evil is undertaken by Christian superheroes who do dramatic things. Some expressed a desire for an over-the-top performance, a drama, a battle of wills or battle for souls. They expected the Church of England to provide the triumph of 'good' over 'evil'. By contacting the 'top powers' some envisaged the Archbishop of Canterbury riding out to battle with a flaming sword, like Gandalf before Minas Tirith defying the forces of Sauron. Others referenced the pain of having superpowers, creating outcasts as in *X-Men*,[52] or the two-edged sword of special abilities as in *Heroes*.[53] To deliver others from evil might entail suffering, sacrifice and exclusion.

Underneath the themes

Each theme has a subtext: a need to frame the question, 'how can we be delivered from evil?', which is how the enquiries come into Church circles. Although the enquirers want to talk about wider theological questions, they are often firmly centred in the 'no religion' category. Notwithstanding, they want to work out how to live their lives through words or practices that will deliver them from a sense of oppression or fear. Many are happy to try prayer and feel strangely listened to, even when they do not believe in any kind of divinity.

Interestingly, some of this contemporary feeling about death and evil has been encapsulated within a strongly humanistic or atheistic idea, or presented as definitely post-Christian and enquirers want to talk about this too. For example, the Ricky Gervais series, *After Life*,[54] features a bereaved person, played by Gervais, who suffers and lashes out, without comfort, except from the kindness and tolerance of others. As you might expect with Gervais, a Christian hope, evinced by an annoying co-worker, is shot down and dismissed in a matter of a few sentences, though Gervais's character finds it in him to lie to a child cancer patient who asks him if he believes in heaven, and much of the examination of his grief takes place in front of his late wife's gravestone where he wonders whether he should have indulged his wife's desire for an afterlife, 'something', more generously.

Theological questions and scenarios are being worked on all the time in popular culture, even in 'Christian' death metal.[55] The problem is that we in the Church often have no mechanisms for engaging with these rich seams of imagination or discovery, debate, and finding out what God is doing there, much less have the capacity to address powerful fears and anxieties that urgently need the care that brings deliverance: the zombies in people's heads. If we want to engage with what 'deliver us from evil' means in popular culture, we have to go to the stories all around us where that question is being probed, argued over and adopted in myriad ways.

References

Anne Richards and Peter Privett (eds), 2009, *Through the Eyes of a Child: new insights in theology from a child's perspective*, London: Church House Publishing.

Garry Young, 2014, *Ethics in the Virtual World: The Morality and Psychology of Gaming*, London and New York: Routledge.

Further reading

Darryl Caterine and John W. Morehead (eds), 2019, *The Paranormal and Popular Culture: A Postmodern Religious Landscape*, Abingdon, Oxon: Routledge.

Jessica Martin, 2020, *Holiness and Desire*, Norwich: Canterbury Press.

Esther Priyadharshini, Jennifer Rowsell, Rebecca Westrup and Victoria Carrington (eds), 2015, *Generation Z: Zombies, Popular Culture and Educating Youth*, Germany: Springer Singapore.

Notes

1 Famed for 'satanic' lyrics, Venom's first release was 'In League with Satan/Live like an Angel' (1981) with studio albums, the influential *Welcome to Hell* (1981), *Black Metal* (1982), *At War with Satan* (1984) and *Possessed* (1985).

2 Pioneers of 'hardgore' or 'splatter death metal', and famed for stomach churning artwork, Carcass is known for albums such as *Reek of Putrefaction* (1988), *Symphonies of Sickness* (1989), *Necroticism – Descanting the Insalubrious* (1991) and *Heartwork* (1993).

3 Deicide is a deeply controversial band which has been banned on a number of occasions for its vividly anti-Christian lyrics and is the creator of albums such as *To Hell with God* (2011), *In the Minds of Evil* (2013) and *Overtures of Blasphemy* (2018).

4 https://deathdoom.com/blog/death-metal/death-metal-lyrics/ (accessed 6.2.24).

5 Described on Rotten Tomatoes as 'A fascinating entry into stories about faith, while not having a self-seriousness to its ideas. The wrath monster trio might be absurd, but the madness within *Hellbound* is extremely believable', https://www.rottentomatoes.com/tv/hellbound/s01 (accessed 6.2.24).

6 https://www.theguardian.com/tv-and-radio/2021/nov/23/south-korean-horror-hellbound-takes-over-squid-game-as-most-popular-netflix-series-globally (accessed 6.2.24),

7 The premise of the *Resident Evil* franchise is humans versus Umbrella Corporation which creates bio-weapons and mutagens which give rise to zombies and monsters which attack humans: 'bioterrorism'.

8 *The Evil Within* features a protagonist who must make his way through a series of nightmare scenarios, facing antagonists such as 'The Haunted' and 'The Sadist'. A mental hospital offers safe haven. 'Madonna' statues offer keys to supplies.

9 *Silent Hill* features individuals who must search for lost, missing, or dead people by entering a twisted, monster-filled reality and engaging with an evil cult. The 'Otherworld', filled with monsters, is supposed to mirror psychological states, feelings and emotions, especially fear, anger or frustration. Player choices matter. Later games in the franchise feature multiple endings based on those choices.

10 *Resident Evil* has been listed as one of the 15 most influential video games of all time.

11 See the Rt Revd Paul Butler's comment in Richards and Privett (2009), p. 243.

12 Drill music is often dark, violent, threatening or nihilistic. It is sometimes associated with gang violence and may be banned, though some argue that moves to ban some drill videos is occasioned by moral panic about its content. Artists include Digga D, Unknown T and Headie One; see: https://www.tuko.co.ke/416261-uk-drill-rappers-20-artists-listen-2021.html (accessed 6.2.24).

13 A range of 'satanic' pornography involving 'demons of lust', occult sex rituals and satanic dressing-up is freely available on the most popular free site, Pornhub. More hardcore satanic pornography offers 'sacrifice' videos.

14 https://www.churchofengland.org/sites/default/files/2018-10/gs1771b-Feb10.pdf (accessed 6.2.24).

15 The *Assassin's Creed* series (2007 onwards) follows individuals in the modern present who can return to relive the memories of their ancestors in historical settings. Assassins set themselves against the

corrupt Templars who appear as historical figures, including Popes. Assassins represent freedom of choice versus order and control of others. Rewards come from divine beings which point the way to objects of great power, such as 'The Apple of Eden'.

16 *MediEvil* (1998) follows the fortunes of a dead warrior called Sir Dan Fortesque who must battle evil monsters in haunted scenarios, collecting their souls in a chalice in order to be redeemed and admitted to the Hall of Heroes as a reward.

17 There can be a difference in gaming between first-person view in which you see what the character sees and third-person view in which you watch your character perform. Immersive first-person view can create a sense of personal injury and damage, whereas watching your character die can be painful and distressing in a different way, because your actions have made this person 'die'. See Young (2014), p. 147.

18 *Final Destination* series of films (2000–2011). See https://www.imdb.com/title/tt0195714/ (accessed 6.2.24).

19 Players often create their own soundtracks for video games and post them on platforms like Spotify where they can be accessed by other gamers to vary or enhance their gaming experience. Many video games have award winning soundtracks of their own and the horror genre has soundtracks intended to inspire fear and suspense and a sense of dread or doom. See: https://morbidlybeautiful.com/horror-video-game-music/ (accessed 6.2.24).

20 *Miracle Workers* (2019–) is a comedy about angels trying to help humans when God intends to destroy the earth. See: https://www.imdb.com/title/tt7529770/ (accessed 6.2.24).

21 *Forever* (2014) is a TV series about an immortal man who works as a medical examiner in a morgue, see https://www.imdb.com/title/tt7529770/ (accessed 6.2.24). Immortality or eternal life as a curse is a thread which runs through various TV series including the character of Clare in *Heroes*, and in *The Good Place*.

22 *The Good Place* (2016–2020); see https://www.imdb.com/title/tt4955642 (accessed 6.2.24).

23 For example, in Iain M. Banks' science fiction novel *Surface Detail* (2010), the narrative follows an attempt to track down and abolish manufactured virtual-reality hells which supply torture and despair to individuals as punishment or as a 'lesson' to keep populations in line.

24 *Squid Game* (2021), see https://www.imdb.com/title/tt10919420/ (accessed 6.2.24).

25 *Good Omens* (2019), see https://www.imdb.com/title/tt1869454/ (accessed 6.2.24).

26 So in Series 13, Episode 4, 'The Village of the Angels' (21 November 2021), enquirers wanted to talk about the shocking capture of the Doctor and her transformation into one of the Weeping Angels.

27 *The Sixth Sense* (1999), see: https://www.imdb.com/title/tt0167404/ (accessed 6.2.24).

28 *The Others* (2001), see: https://www.imdb.com/title/tt0230600/ (accessed 6.2.24).

29 J. K. Rowling, *Harry Potter*, books 1–7 (London: Bloomsbury, 1997–2007) and feature films 1–8 (2001–2011), see https://www.imdb.com/title/tt0241527/ (accessed 6.2.24). There is current controversy (2022) about the video game *Harry Potter Legacy* as to whether spells of torture (the Unforgiveable Curses) will be included in the game and available for children to use, see https://www.hogwartslegacy.com/en-gb#:~:text=Hogwarts%20Legacy%20is%20an%20immersive,adventure%20in%20the%20wizarding%20world (accessed 6.2.24).

30 https://www.theatlantic.com/health/archive/2015/10/life-among-the-vampires/413446/ (accessed 6.2.24).

31 See point 8 at https://www.paranormalinvestigationuk.com/paranormal-help (accessed 6.2.24).

32 Skin-walkers are associated with Navajo narratives and typically

represent a malevolent entity which can disguise itself as an animal. They are currently populating TikTok; see: https://www.dazeddigital. com/life-culture/article/50931/1/skinwalkers-the-creepy-creatures-terrifying-tiktok (accessed 6.2.24).

33 See Steve Taylor, 2018, "'Religious Piety and Pigs' Brains": The Faith of Zombies in Burr Steers's Pride and Prejudice and Zombies', https://jasna.org/publications-2/persuasions-online/volume-38-no-3/ taylor/ (accessed 6.2.24).

34 *The Walking Dead* (2010–2022), see https://www.imdb.com/title/ tt1520211/ (accessed 6.2.24).

35 *Twilight* (2008) is an adaptation from a series about human-vampire romance by Stephanie Meyer, https://www.imdb.com/title/ tt1099212/ (accessed 6.2.24).

36 *Independence Day* (1996) – aliens arrive, destroy cities and tell humans that all they want is for them to die. The battle for the planet brings disparate people together and leadership and self-sacrifice enable the triumph of 'good' over the alien 'evil', https://www.imdb.com/title/ tt0116629/ (accessed 6.2.24).

37 *Aliens* (1986) is the second in a series of sci-fi horror films in which monsters try to hunt and annihilate humans, using them as hosts for reproduction, https://www.imdb.com/title/tt0090605/ (accessed 6.2.24).

38 Spoken by Kyle Reese, sent back from the future to protect Sarah, the mother of the saviour John Connor, against the determined murderous Terminator who has come back in time to kill her, *The Terminator* (1984), https://www.imdb.com/title/tt0088247/ (accessed 6.2.24).

39 *Battlestar Galactica* (2004–2009) has a rump of humans fleeing through space looking for a Promised Land, pursued by fanatically religious androids, the Cylons, who can appear human, https://www. imdb.com/title/tt0407362/ (accessed 6.2.24).

40 *Star Wars* (1977–) is a franchise telling the story of a motley crew of humans, other creatures and droids, fighting against the evil 'Empire' guided by the mysterious Force.

41 *Dune* (1984/2021) is an adaptation of Frank Herbert's sci-fi classic about a noble family trying to protect the universe's most precious commodity and its planet from the hands of evil powers who wish to dominate and destroy, https://www.imdb.com/title/tt1160419/ (accessed 6.2.24).

42 *Westworld* (2016) is a theme park filled with androids that can be used by humans for any desire or fantasy they choose. It contains themes of exploitation and suffering and the search for liberation and salvation, https://www.imdb.com/title/tt0475784/ (accessed 6.2.24).

43 In Harlan Ellison's classic story 'I Have No Mouth and I Must Scream', a sentient computer called AM kills all humans except for a final few which it takes into itself, announces its utter contempt and hatred for biological beings, and tortures the last survivor for eternity. A similar theme is played out in the prequels to Frank Herbert's classic *Dune*.

44 *Love Island* (2015–) is a dating show and in 2018 was the most watched show in ITV2's history. It generates huge social media debate and discussion, and also controversy about contestants who have later died by suicide, https://www.imdb.com/title/tt14230710/ (accessed 6.2.24).

45 *The Lovely Bones* (2009) from Alice Sebold's novel centres on a murdered girl in a kind of purgatory, looking back at the world and weighing vengeance for her murder against peace for her grieving family, https://www.imdb.com/title/tt0380510/ (accessed 6.2.24).

46 In *Ashes to Ashes* (2008), dead police officers have to work out their issues before they can pass on to the next life, but their souls are pulled between an unlikely angelic and a demonic presence in the department, https://www.imdb.com/title/tt1008108/ (accessed 6.2.24).

47 *Lost* (2004–2010) is about a group of people in a plane crash on an

island where they have to work out the meaning of their lives and pasts only to discover (finally) that they are all dead. See: https://www.imdb.com/title/tt0411008/ (accessed 6.2.24).

48 In *Lucifer* (2016–2021), Lucifer Morningstar leaves hell to come to LA and help police catch and punish criminals using his devilish powers, https://www.imdb.com/title/tt4052886/ (accessed 6.2.24).

49 *Constantine* (2005) has an exorcist and demonologist help a police officer prove her sister's suicide was not what it seemed, https://www.imdb.com/title/tt0360486/ (accessed 6.2.24).

50 In *Dexter* (2006–2013), a serial killer works for the police department, murdering other murderers according to his particular moral code, https://www.imdb.com/title/tt0773262/ (accessed 6.2.24).

51 *Hellboy* (2019) features Hellboy, the son of a fallen angel who ends up on Earth and now protects from mysterious threats, https://www.imdb.com/title/tt2274648/ (accessed 6.2.24).

52 In *X-Men* (2000), mutants with superpowers are excluded and discriminated against. Two rival groups of mutants clash over the use and abuse of their powers, https://www.imdb.com/title/tt0120903/ (accessed 6.2.24).

53 In *Heroes* (2006–2010), people with superpowers are pursued by evil Sylar who desires to murder them and take their powers from them so he can become the ultimate human, https://www.imdb.com/title/tt0813715/ (accessed 6.2.24).

54 *After Life* (2019–2022), https://www.imdb.com/title/tt8398600/ (accessed 6.2.24).

55 https://www.thegospelcoalition.org/article/metal-lyrics-psalms-lament/ (accessed 6.2.24); https://tif.ssrc.org/2010/08/19/pipeline-to-god/ (accessed 6.2.24).

3

The Ministry of Deliverance in the Twentieth Century: Lessons for Contemporary Practice

Nick Ladd

Introduction

On one occasion, while praying with a person who was dealing with deep relational hurt, they became aware of an oppressive presence in them that was somehow attached to the wounds of their life. As we slowly prayed through the pain and brokenness, they reached a point of wanting to be released from this presence – which we did – bringing a level of release and freedom, which needed to be seen to be appreciated. This would not have been resolved by prayer and counsel alone and this is why deliverance ministry is so important.

At the same time, we are only too aware of the dangers of immature, careless or ignorant attempts at ministry. Sally Nash in her book, *Shame and the Church* writes that 'one of the topics that evoked the strongest opinions was people's experience of healing and deliverance' with one of her correspondents commenting, 'I was once told that I didn't have just one demon but a whole hotel of them' (2020, p. 81). I found similar experiences in my research on mental health and church life (Ladd 2020, p. 177). Careless pastoral ministry is always deeply problematic, but it becomes more so where it pertains to beliefs towards which the wider culture is broadly incredulous, even where there are layers of interest and fascination.

The Ministry of Deliverance in the Twentieth Century

In this chapter, I argue that the multi-vocal journey with the practice of deliverance during the twentieth century can be understood as the Church's attempt to wrestle with and to be authentic to the Gospel in modern culture. Furthermore, that there is something to be learned from conflicts and convergences around this ministry and the potential for healthy integration of difference to generate a more rounded ministry. Such integration is a mark of maturity, which in turn has implications for safe practice.

I take a practical theology approach – theological reflection on experience. The advantage of this is that it can give voice to ordinary practitioners who might otherwise be unheard. Moreover, the nature of deliverance ministry is such that most people come to it because of experiences in practice that disrupt prior assumptions. I conducted a small-scale and informal survey of clergy and laity, but would like to broaden it.[1] Of the 74 people contacted, the vast majority said that they had been called upon to minister to people and in places; a few of them often, most sometimes or rarely. Only four said they had never been called upon for either ministry. I have correlated this practice base with Church of England reports and writing by practitioners in the same period as well as more historical and critically reflective writing that has emerged since 2000.

However, practical theological approaches can reify experience in ways that give little room for critique. Just as academics need to hear the stories of practitioners, so practitioners need to be open to critical reflection and dialogue. My aim here is to narrate this practice, but also to raise questions, propose areas where interdisciplinary dialogue might be helpful, and make suggestions about future needs if practice is to develop healthily and safely. A mature approach will encourage all involved both to attend carefully to views that are different, but also to assert their own perspectives with courage and respect. In the process, attention needs to be given to those voices that easily go unheard.

Finally a word about the boundaries of this chapter. My world is that of the Anglican Church and the Charismatic Movement in the UK, though I have widened my reading to include Pentecostal and Roman Catholic writers. I have no detailed knowledge of other cultural perspectives within the UK and neither do most of those I surveyed, except where they have been immersed in different cultural worlds through ministry overseas. It is important that what I write here be complemented by research on practice of ministry from non-Western perspectives in the UK.

Deliverance in historical perspective

For those who have been involved with deliverance ministry, it is easy to assume it has been with us forever. However, evidence suggests that the practice was rare in the early centuries of Anglicanism, particularly after the promulgation of Canon 72 in 1604 which prohibited exercise of the ministry without episcopal license.[2]

In the twentieth century, there were two points where deliverance ministry received fresh impetus – the 1920s and the 1970s (Young 2018, pp. 93–107; Collins 2009, pp. 41–56). Arguably, in the first case, the debate over spiritualism that ran from the mid-nineteenth to the early twentieth centuries created the intellectual space to explore demonology (Byrne 2010). The second was most obviously driven by what many describe as the 'occult explosion' in the 50s and 60s alongside the burgeoning Charismatic movement with its deep awareness of spiritual realities and experiences (Buzzard 1976, pp. 17–8; Collins 2009, pp. 40–80; Richards 1974, pp. 19–37; Young 2018, p. 131).

From the 1920s to the 1960s, Anglican ministry was shaped particularly by Anglo-Catholics, Gilbert Shaw and Dom Robert Petitpierre, the latter being very influential in the work for the 1964 report commissioned by the Bishop of Exeter in the light of growing requests for exorcism (Young 2018, pp. 102–30). This work went further than previous reports in describing and contextualizing the ministry of exorcism – offering a range of prayers and liturgies from Roman Catholic sources (Petitpierre 1972, pp. 29–46). The report recommended the appointment of an exorcist in each diocese and proposed centres of training in each province. Its safeguarding proposals were, however, somewhat less rigorous than those of the 1958 Archbishops' Commission that preceded it (p. 25).

Despite some eccentric practitioners over the years, it is possible to trace from these early practitioners a thoughtful and measured Anglican practice through the later decades of the twentieth century, especially with the formation of the Christian Exorcism Study Group, latterly the Christian Deliverance Study Group. Their propensity to 'work quietly', as they put it, means that their presence has not been well-known in the wider Church – a point that I will return to as I consider the next development in the ministry (Perry 1987, p. 1).

The Charismatic movement had its antecedents in the Pentecostal movement at the turn of the century, which in turn had given birth to the post-war healing revival in the 1940s and 1950s, with its emphasis on deliverance ministry (Collins 2009, pp. 24–41). Something I notice that no-one seems to have commented on is the rise of this ministry subsequent to both world wars in the twentieth century.

Though there are many highly influential Pentecostal practitioners, for Anglican Charismatics, the development of the ministries of healing and deliverance was mediated in the 1980s and 1990s mainly through the ministry of Vineyard leader, John Wimber. Wimber made a fuller attempt than many practitioners to theologize his approach and I will draw on this to articulate the strengths and weaknesses of Anglican Charismatic practice.

Anglican Charismatics, for the most part, were unaware of a parallel tradition within the wider Anglican Church and like most adolescent movements it was impatient with what it assumed to be the cautious, even unspiritual, practice of the Mother Church. Anglican practitioners, however, were more than aware of Charismatic practices and tended to conclude that they were dangerous and unhelpful (Young 2018, p. 172). The journey of the later twentieth century has been marked by a certain rapprochement and mutual learning (Collins 2009, pp. 187–97). In *this* century, it is notable that there has been little writing about the *practice* of the ministry but a certain amount of critical and historical reflection upon it. This suggests that we are at a good point for a contribution to redrawing the practice for the twenty-first century.

Deliverance ministry as a theological and spiritual journey within modernity

Practice is theologically and contextually freighted. Through our practice, we discover and express our theological and spiritual commitments, which are drawn from our traditions and experience but also shaped in the cultural world – or perhaps better a social imaginary – in which we live and breathe. The way we live this out differs according to the way these various influences come together in our personal and communal living.

Anglican practitioners, with a strong theology of Creation, tend to have an open and affirming approach to the culture in which they live, even as they are aware of the tensions that are generated by the interplay of culture and theological traditions. So, for example, they are open and enquiring towards paranormal experiences, rather than instinctively rejecting it as evil as more conservative practitioners would do (Perry 1987, p. 48; Young 2018, p. 111).

Modernity in the early and mid-twentieth century was deeply sceptical of the 'supernatural'. When the shocking impact of exorcism gone wrong in the 'Barnsley case' hit the headlines in 1975, it generated an immediate theological backlash from Anglican liberal theologians, withdrawal from deliverance ministry by the Church of Scotland and deep caution from the Methodist Church (Church of Scotland 1976;

Methodist Division of Social Responsibility 1976; Twelftree 1985, pp. 11–16). The Church of England, by contrast, was more measured in its response, seeking rather to create parameters for safe practice, without rejecting the ministry out of hand (Archbishop of York's Study Group 1974).

From the 1920s, there was already a recognition of the importance of an interdisciplinary approach – particularly psychiatric and psychological perspectives – and this became stronger as the decades unfolded in response in particular to scepticism and caution about 'supernatural' diagnoses. Perry interweaves both perspectives (1987 pp. 71–97). A psychological approach tends to look both for problems and solutions within rather than external to the person and there was growing conviction in Anglican practice that much spiritual disturbance in both places and people was more typically a sign of inner psychological disturbance and should be treated accordingly. For example, most practitioners have concluded that poltergeist experiences should be understood in terms of inner psychological disturbance of someone in the household and therefore the appropriate response is pastoral care and healing prayer rather than deliverance (Bray 2020, pp. 1–16; Perry 1987, pp. 12–26; Walker 1997, pp. 17–22). This accords with my experience. Respondents talked about how calls to disturbances in houses frequently revealed hurt and brokenness in people, rooted in personal or relational turmoil and pain, such as bereavement, relational breakdown, mental health challenges or traumatic experiences; this was true also in my experience when part of a diocesan deliverance team.

However, within literature and practice, there is the recognition of an irreducible minimum of cases, with both places and people, which are inexplicable in purely psychological terms (Perry 1987, p. 82). Though from Perry in 1987 through Walker in 1997 and onto *Time to Heal* in 2000, this aspect becomes more and more attenuated, leading some respondents to complain that there is little or no spiritual dimension in the training that they receive for this ministry.

Charismatic deliverance ministry, by contrast, began with a very different relationship to the culture. Practitioners write about how their experiences of the Spirit – and specifically healing and deliverance ministry – completely overturned their modern liberal assumptions and led them to a transformation of worldview, which was more in line with Christians in the non-Western world (Basham 1972, pp. 51–6; Dow 1990, p. 4; Linn 1981, pp. 5–11; Wimber and Stringer 1986, pp. 42–52).

Wimber articulated this as a rediscovery of the 'supernatural' dimension of reality to which the modern mind was closed through its rational scepticism. The 'supernatural realm' was the place where God's miraculous presence was to be felt and Wimber considered that he had constantly to emphasize this dimension as he, along with most other Charismatics, believed that this was a loss to the Western Church of huge magnitude (1985, pp. 74–96). This could lead him to be dismissive of the 'natural' dimension of life – for example being derisive about a prayer to 'guide the surgeon's hands' as the limit of Christian faith for healing.

In this 'supernatural' ministry, Wimber was guided by a reading of George Ladd's Kingdom theology to posit two realms – the Kingdom of God and the Kingdom of darkness. In ministry terms, everything was a manifestation of one or the other (1985, pp. 13–43). For this reason, Wimber, along with many other Charismatics saw 'demonization' as extremely prevalent (1986, pp. 136–8; Basham 1972, pp. 187–95). This was an unhealthy dualism, the 'paranoid kingdom' as Andrew Walker named it, and led Wimber and others away from God's presence in ordinary human experience. Ironically, his Nature/Supernature dualism was more a product of enlightenment thinking than he realized (1985, pp. 86–8).

Wimber had careful and thorough guidelines for the discernment of the need for deliverance and he would often say that many cases that purported to be demonization were nothing of the kind. However, because of his disinterest in the 'natural', he does not ask whether the symptoms of 'demonization' he describes could also be interpreted in psychological or psychiatric terms; others follow the same path in the narration of their ministry stories (1986, pp. 240–4; Basham 1972, pp. 137–40).

Charismatic spirituality was deeply suspicious of and at odds with modernity and generated a counter-cultural and potentially ghettoized way of life. Nevertheless, it pinpointed a spiritual deficit in modernity, which is pertinent to deliverance ministry. Respondents were clear that not all could be explained in terms of human psychology and, particularly, but not exclusively, in the case of occult involvement, repentance, renunciation and setting free was necessary – deliverance ministry. Charismatic ministry, for all its flaws, has kept that reality front and centre.

Collins (2009, pp. 195–6) writes about the 'routinization' in the twenty-first century of what he considers the unhealthy 'enthusiasm' of the Charismatic movement and a move from the 'power encounter' to the 'truth encounter', exemplified in the ministry of Roman Catholic layman, Neal Lozano (2009, pp. 11–21). While, I agree with Collins estimation of the 'faddism' and immaturity of much Charismatic practice, I see this later development more as a process of maturation than the waning of a movement. To place deliverance ministry in the context of a process of self-examination, spiritual accompaniment and healing prayer seems to me to be a healthier and more balanced approach. Wimber actually paved the way for this through his emphasis on inner healing ministry. Respondents consistently placed this ministry within the context of prayers for peace and healing, even if few of them ever took it much further in terms of specific prayers of deliverance. In my experience, unnecessary drama arises in this ministry when the roots of the oppression – whether personal or social – are not attended to in partnership with those to whom they minister, causing pain and distress that are easily avoided. Deliverance ministry sits much more safely and meaningfully within a wider process of pastoral transformation.

So the question before us in the light of these different cultural articulations is: what does it mean to have a theologically informed and mature ministry of deliverance that is appropriate for and appropriately challenging of our cultural context? In the final part of this paper, I want to make some suggestions and ask some questions.

Shaping a healthy practice of deliverance

I have been arguing that our approach to deliverance ministry is shaped by the interplay in practice between our spiritual and theological convictions and the social world in which we live. I want to proceed now to explore how that journey in the twentieth century might inform our practice today.

Language and culture

First, there has been a journey in the way language is used. Most respondents were uncomfortable with the word 'exorcism' and preferred the word 'deliverance' – but added that they would be very cautious about using any such language in pastoral conversation. The cultural reasons for this were noted, especially in relation to the portrayal of exorcism in popular culture and film. But there were other reasons – not least that deliverance was a broader, more open and less freighted word and allowed people to place the ministry in a wider pastoral and healing context. However, one or two felt that the breadth of the word deliverance was unhelpful and that there was a specific, if rare, situation in which exorcism was the correct word to describe accurately what was needed.

The same goes for the word 'possession'. Respondents were concerned with the implied obliteration of human agency in a way that is both untrue and unhelpful. I have certainly found even in the most extreme cases, that there has always been some level of the human self both present and recognizable. Though, there is evidence both in spiritual and medical practice for the possibility of a deep attenuation of that sense of self.

Therapy, liberation and deliverance ministry

Lying behind this debate about language is our culture's preference for immanent rather than transcendent explanations, something Charles Taylor argues shapes psychiatric interpretation of human distress (Cook 2013, pp. 141–59). Pattison adds to this a challenge to the dominance of therapeutic individualism in pastoral care, arguing that this underwrites unawareness of social injustice (1997, pp. 208–20; 2000, pp. 82–105).

Attending to socio-political reality can help us to read Gospel accounts of exorcism in different ways. Myers argues that Mark frames the early part of his Gospel with two accounts of exorcism – one that focuses on oppression by the religious leadership (Mark 1.21–28) and the other, oppression from the occupying Roman powers (Mark 5.1–20). He suggests that the interplay of the seen and unseen worlds in biblical eschatology allows us to see these stories as descriptions of spiritual oppression reflected and expressed in political and economic guise (Myers 2008, pp. 190–4).[3] Respondents said that they had many more calls for deliverance ministry when they worked in more socially deprived areas – something that has been my experience also.

We understand the strengths of immanent interpretation in therapeutic work in terms of the way it encourages ownership, responsibility and agency – and that this is a key factor in human growth and maturation. However, resistance to the idea of external forces may contribute to unawareness of the impact of more systemic problems and the way in which evil forces may exploit this through human suffering and injustice. Recognizing the importance of immanence does not rule out the possibility of addressing external forces that are 'other' to the person; I have certainly seen the impact of such prayer in a way that does not abrogate the agency of the person prayed for.

Underlying this interpretation is an important question about biblical interpretation. Charismatic practitioners tend to read the Bible literally and so believe in the reality of demons who possess both will and power, which tends towards an individualized ministry (Dow 1990, p. 7; Wimber and Stringer 1986, pp. 112–20).

A metaphorical reading like Myers still makes room for the reality of evil but allows for a more complex reading of the relationship of the personal and the socio-political (Wa Gatuma 2011, pp. 220–42). Many respondents preferred such language.

Of course, when the interpretation becomes mythological, then the tendency is for deliverance ministry to dissipate altogether (Wright 2011, pp. 203–21). Discussion around the way we read the Bible for and in our culture seems very important in framing this ministry for the twenty-first century.

The preference of our culture for immanent, therapeutic interpretation of distress and its scepticism about 'supernatural' perspectives, should not cause us to retreat from the challenge of spiritual discernment. Practitioners and Church of England reports give very careful attention to spiritual diagnosis and good practice and there is much wisdom to be gleaned here. The challenge of discerning accurately should make us cautious and provisional about our diagnoses, but not retreat from them. After all, both medical and psychiatric practice recognize the necessity and inevitability of trial and error in effective diagnosis (Charry 1997, pp. 10–16; White 1976, pp. 283–4). Mainstream Anglican approaches have been careful to take an interdisciplinary approach to deliverance ministry, but one that sometimes fights shy of the possibility of objective spiritual oppression. For all its weaknesses, the Charismatic movement has held onto this reality, though needs to recognize more fully the importance of other perspectives and readings of deliverance ministry. Both, I suggest, need to pay more attention to the social and political dimensions of the ministry.

Conclusion: maturity and safe practice

My argument in this paper is that the twentieth-century journey with deliverance ministry evidences the Church's attempt to find an authentic approach within the reality of the modern world. I have argued that those whose theology encourages them to embrace their culture have worked effectively to create an interdisciplinary approach to this ministry, which nevertheless may have a tendency to attenuate the very real spiritual dimensions of the ministry.

On the other hand, those who have been more critical of modern culture have generated an approach that, while unhelpfully oblivious to more immanent interpretations of human distress, has at the same time championed the reality of the Gospel's power to release people from the thrall of evil – however this is conceptualized.

Twelftree argues that the approach to deliverance in the New Testament was extremely varied from those who embraced a ministry of exorcism to those who saw the battle with evil more in terms of resistance to sin (2011, p. 68). We should not be surprised to find the same traditions appropriately and inappropriately expressed within the contemporary Church. A mature approach will come to the debate to attend closely to the perspective of others, while unafraid to assert with respect one's own understanding. Furthermore, it means coming with openness to change, to create and integrate new understanding together.

Furthermore, both traditions need to pay attention more to the social and political dimensions of this ministry – looking towards social as well as personal transformation, attending to the vulnerabilities present both for those ministering and those ministered to. Taking seriously a liberational perspective also requires careful attention to the agency of those receiving ministry and a recognition – as with any healthy pastoral ministry – of the co-creative nature of such ministry, even where people's personal challenges may seem immense.

This invites the development of a mature ministry which is

most obviously explored within a robust training and mentoring environment. However, over 50 per cent of respondents had received no training or mentoring, and those that had reported a mixed experience. Some found their mentoring very empowering, others the opposite. Some found training restrictive, others inspiring. The training that was most appreciated was that where different traditions and approaches, psychological and spiritual, were brought together in dialogue and mutual respect – a mark of a mature approach. I valued the mentoring I received from Charismatic practitioners who helped me to appreciate the reality of spiritual oppression and build confidence in the power of Christ to bring freedom. I also valued the broad training I received at Anglican regional conferences, especially in helping me to understand more fully the psychological aspects of deliverance ministry.

Most dioceses have teams to oversee this ministry in which such mentoring and training could take place (Perry 1987, pp. 115–19). However, experience of these varies from those that support and empower local clergy in growing in this ministry to those who are controlling and disempowering; again it takes maturity to release the agency of others.

Though it is good that people work in teams, those who carry this level of responsibility ought also to have supervision in the same way that counsellors do. Ideally this should be with someone who, though sympathetic to the ministry, does not share the same presuppositions, so as to avoid the creation of an echo chamber – another mark of maturity. Such supervision should pay attention to the maturity of practice – one that respects and enables the agency, responsibility and ownership of the ministry for the one being prayed for: attending to the inner journey of maturation, even while being alert to the need for appropriate release and freedom from external spiritual forces.

These aims are not easy to achieve. I suggest that ensuring safe and healthy practice is more likely to be achieved by attending to the development and maturity of those in ministry than by creating some form of bureaucratic tick-box approach (Young 2018, pp. 167–70). But the Church should expect and ensure a maturity of approach and practice from those involved in the ministry – people who recognize the dangers of abuse and who are committed to the agency of those to whom they minister. There is a real contribution to be made here from those who have sought to integrate Charismatic and psychological perspectives both in relation to Church of England practice, but also in dialogue with those churches who are finding it hard to integrate safely their traditional thinking in the culture of modernity in which they find themselves.

References

Archbishops' Commission, 1958, *The Church's Ministry of Healing*, London: Church Information Board.

Archbishops' Council, 2000, *A Time to Heal: A Report for the House of Bishops on the Healing Ministry*, London: Church House Publishing.

Archbishop of York's Study Group, 1974, *The Christian Ministry of Healing and Deliverance*, York: Diocese of York.

Don Basham, 1972, *Deliver us from Evil*, London: Hodder & Stoughton.

Jason Bray, 2020, *Deliverance: Everyday Investigations into Poltergeists, Ghosts and other Supernatural Phenomena by an Anglican Priest*, London: Coronet.

L. R. Buzzard, 1976, 'Introduction', in John W. Montgomery, (ed.). *Demon Possession*, Minneapolis, MN: Bethany House Publishers, pp. 17–23.

Georgina Byrne, 2010, *Modern Spiritualism and the Church of England 1850-1939*, Woodbridge: Boydell & Brewer.

Ellen T. Charry, 1997, *By the Renewing of your Minds: The Pastoral Function of Christian Doctrine*, Oxford: Oxford University Press

Church of Scotland, 1976, *Report of the Working Party on Parapsychology*.

James M. Collins, 2009, *Exorcism and Deliverance Ministry in the Twentieth Century*, Milton Keynes: Paternoster.

Christopher C. H. Cook, 2013, 'Transcendence, Immanence and Mental Health', in Christopher C. H. Cook (ed.), *Spirituality, Theology and Mental Health*, London: SCM Press, pp. 141–59.

Graham Dow, 1990, *Those Tiresome Intruders: Sharing Experience in the Ministry of Deliverance*, Grove Pastoral Series 41, Nottingham: Grove Books Ltd.

Nick M. Ladd, 2020, 'The Formation of Christian Community: Reading Scripture in the Light of Mental Health', in Christopher C. H. Cook and Isabelle Hamley (eds), *The Bible and Mental Health*, London: SCM Press, pp. 173–91.

Matthew Linn, 1981, 'My Doubts about Evil Spirits', in Matthew Linn and Dennis Linn, *Deliverance Prayer*, New York, NY: Paulist Press, pp. 5–15.

Neal Lozano, 2009, *Resisting the Devil: A Catholic Perspective on Deliverance*, Huntingdon, IN: Our Sunday Visitor Inc.

Methodist Division of Social Responsibility, 1976, *A Methodist Statement on Exorcism*, London: The Methodist Conference.

Ched Myers, 2008, *Binding the Strong Man: A Political Reading of Mark's Story of Jesus*, Maryknoll, NY: Orbis Books.

Sally Nash, 2020, *Shame and the Church: Exploring and Transforming Practice*, London: SCM Press

Stephen Pattison, 1997, *Pastoral Care and Liberation Theology*, London: SPCK.

Stephen Pattison, 2000, *A Critique of Pastoral Care*, London: SCM Press.

Dom Robert Petitpierre (ed.), 1972, *Exorcism: The Report of a Commission Convened by the Bishop of Exeter*, London: SPCK,

Michael Perry (ed.), 1987, *Deliverance: Psychic Disturbances and Occult Involvement*, London: SPCK.

John Richards, 1974, *But Deliver Us from Evil*, London: Darton, Longman & Todd Ltd.

Graham H. Twelftree, 1985, *Christ Triumphant: Exorcism Then and Now*, London: Hodder & Stoughton.

Graham H. Twelftree, 2011, 'Deliverance and Exorcism in the New Testament', in William K. Kay and Robin Parry (eds), *Exorcism and Deliverance: Multi-Disciplinary Studies*, Milton Keynes: Paternoster, pp. 45–68.

Kabiro Wa Gatumu, 2011, 'Deliverance and Exorcism in Theological Perspective: 2. Possession and Exorcism as New Testament Evidence for a Theology of Christ's Supremacy', in William K. Kay and Robin Parry (eds), *Exorcism and Deliverance: Multi-Disciplinary Studies*, Milton Keynes: Paternoster, pp. 222–42.

Dominic Walker, 1997, *The Ministry of Deliverance*, London: Darton, Longman & Todd Ltd.

J. White, 1976, 'Problems and Procedures in Exorcism', in John W. Montgomery (ed.), *Demon Possession*, Minneapolis, MN: Bethany House Publishers, pp. 281–99.

John Wimber and Kevin Springer, 1985, *Power Evangelism*, London: Hodder & Stoughton.

John Wimber and Kevin Springer, 1986, *Power Healing*, London: Hodder & Stoughton.

Nigel G. Wright, 2011, 'Deliverance and Exorcism in Theological Perspective: 1. Is there any Substance to Evil?', in William K. Kay and Robin Parry (eds), *Exorcism and Deliverance: Multi-Disciplinary Studies*, Milton Keynes: Paternoster, pp. 203–21.

Francis Young, 2018, *A History of Anglican Exorcism: Deliverance and Demonology in Church Ritual*, London: I. B. Tauris.

Notes

1 I contacted 66 clergy, some of whom forwarded this to a further eight making 74 in all. I had 38 clergy responses. I also sent it to 21 lay people and received five responses. It was also forwarded by two other contacts to a network of health chaplains and a network of volunteer chaplains. I have no idea of the size of these groups or how many of the chaplaincy responses that I received came from either of these groups. Respondents' experience of ministry varied from 18 months to 54 years. Even though five people had forwarded the survey to their diocesan lead, there were still a further eight in the sample who were part of diocesan deliverance teams; clearly the Church of England has a wealth of practical experience to call upon to understand the present state of this ministry. There were a few who said that a survey did not give them the flexibility to say all the things they would have liked to and, if the Church wants to continue researching this in more depth, it would be possible to broaden and deepen the survey outcomes with some in-depth one-to-one interviews.

2 Canon 72 was rescinded in 1969.

3 I am indebted to Andii Bowsher for drawing my attention to Myers.

4

Deliverance in Practice:
Mental Health, Theology and
Professional Boundaries

Christopher C. H. Cook

People may seek deliverance ministry for a variety of reasons. Some matters are dealt with easily and fall within the range of ordinary pastoral care. Others are more complex and not so easily addressed. The use of the vocabulary of deliverance, the paranormal or the demonic, and the presentation to church rather than healthcare for help, is in itself significant and may guide in understanding how people perceive their problems and the kind of help that they are looking for. Within this broader domain there are those who have a history and/or diagnosis of mental disorder.

There are many documented cases in the published literature that indicate a connection between demon possession and mental disorder (e.g. Yap 1960; Whitwell and Barker 1980; Hale and Pinninti 1994). However, there are many reasons why someone may seek help from a priest rather than a mental health professional, ranging from lack of general knowledge about mental health problems, or fear of mental health professionals, through to lack of personal insight, or strong beliefs about the spiritual nature of the problem.

Those tasked by bishops with the provision of deliverance ministry are primarily clergy and generally do not have clinical expertise on matters of mental health. Questions therefore arise at the boundaries of pastoral and clinical domains of expertise concerning good professional practice. Given the vulnerability of those concerned, and the potential for deliverance ministry to cause harm if conducted in an insensitive or ill-considered manner, these questions are both practical and important.

In this context, the present chapter seeks to explore more exactly what the medical contribution to deliverance ministry might be and what it looks like in the context of currently available guidance on good medical practice.

Medical involvement in deliverance in the Church of England: a brief history

In 1958, in a report of the Archbishops' Commission on *The Church's Ministry of Healing*, an appendix devoted to exorcism acknowledged that a difficulty was presented by the different use of language in relation to exorcism by those from theological and medical backgrounds. Concern was also expressed about the possible misuse of exorcism:

> It must be recognized, therefore, that there is a danger in the misuse of exorcism, and the patient must be carefully examined, both medically and spiritually, the doctor and the priest working in close collaboration. (The Archbishops' Commission 1958, p. 78)

The report recommended the setting up of an advisory panel of priests and doctors to which cases might be referred by a bishop 'for diagnosis', but the panel was never set up and the process was never implemented (Young 2018, p. 117).

In 1972, in the findings of a commission convened by the Bishop of Exeter, it was recommended that before an exorcism is undertaken 'the case should be referred by [a] general practitioner to a competent physician in psychological medicine' (Petitpierre 1972, p. 23). Thus, diagnosis (and implicitly treatment) of a possible mental or physical illness should precede exorcism.

In 1974, after being exorcized at St Thomas' church in Barnsley, and with apparent disregard to recommendations such as those made in Exeter, a man called Michael Taylor returned home and murdered his wife. Taylor was subsequently found not guilty by reason of insanity and was committed to the secure psychiatric facility at Broadmoor (Young 2018, pp. 142–46).

Guidelines from the House of Bishops, issued in 1975, recommended that deliverance ministry be undertaken 'in collaboration with the resources of medicine', but no detail was offered concerning the nature of this collaboration or the specific 'resources of medicine' that might be important (Young 2018, p. 154). These guidelines were reiterated and endorsed in the report of a working party on the ministry of healing, chaired by the Bishop of Chelmsford and presented to the House of Bishops, published in 2000 under the title *A Time to Heal* (Working Party on Healing 2000, pp. 168, 355).

In 2012, a revision of the 1975 guidelines expanded a little upon the guidance previously provided and suggested:

- A multi-disciplinary approach is to be desired, consulting and collaborating as necessary with doctors, psychologists and psychiatrists, and recognizing that health-care professionals and related agencies are bound by codes of conduct.
- In relation to counselling and psychotherapy, it was noted that these should only be provided by suitably accredited counsellors and therapists.

For reasons that are not clear, the recommendation for collaboration with the resources of medicine moved from first in the 1975 list to third in the 2012 list.

In 2017 another revision of the guidelines was undertaken and circulated to bishops but was never published.

In safeguarding guidance published online by the Church of England in 2021, working and consultation with 'medical practitioners, psychologists and psychiatrists; is set out as a key requirement for deliverance ministry (4.1.2).[1] In this guidance, it is further required that these professionals should be 'employed by (and thus accountable to) local health services and will be bound by their own codes of professional conduct'. However, in a footnote that is somewhat contradictory of this statement, it is said: 'There may be circumstances where the mental health professional is not in local health service employment, but is in private practice or academia. In these circumstances, they must be members of the appropriate professional body, e.g. Royal College of Psychiatrists or British Psychological Association.' Safeguarding guidance further stipulates that 'a medical professional must be consulted, and all issues of consent, capability and ongoing safeguarding actions must be discussed with that person'. In respect of deliverance ministry with children, the rite must have been authorized by the bishop after consultation with the Diocesan Safeguarding Advisor and a 'medical professional'.

We know little about how these guidelines have been implemented over the years, but there is reason to believe that practice has varied from one diocese to another. Some dioceses have issued their own guidelines for deliverance ministry, raising questions as to how diocesan and national policy sit alongside each other. Local congregations have also varied in how they have followed, adapted, or disregarded, the guidelines.

Professional accountability, boundaries and safeguarding

Earlier guidance from the House of Bishops was very vague, although it must be recognized that it was originally formulated half a century ago and the concept of safeguarding as we now know it was not to emerge until several decades later. On the other hand, the safeguarding guidance issued in 2021 raises more questions about professional accountability, indemnity, roles, boundaries and responsibilities than it answers. For example, it would appear very unlikely that any involvement with deliverance ministry would be construed as being within an NHS contract of employment, except perhaps in circumstances where a doctor was approached by a member of a deliverance ministry team to discuss the possibility of providing deliverance ministry to his/her patient. To whom, then, is a medical professional accountable if they are engaged in deliverance ministry in a church, and not a healthcare, context? References to 'medical practitioners, psychologists and psychiatrists' provide a helpful catch-all, but do not show awareness of the different skills and expertise of these professionals, nor is it clear exactly what they are respectively being asked to contribute to deliverance ministry.

To whom, then, should the convener of a deliverance ministry team turn for help, in what circumstances, and with what questions in mind? Supposing that a member of a parish congregation happens to be a medical professional, how should he/she respond if asked for advice and to what extent should he/she become involved in the actual exercise of deliverance ministry? Implicitly, it would seem, the central questions arising are those of diagnosis and treatment of mental disorders but, somewhat surprisingly, this is nowhere made explicit in any of the guidance offered to date. Supposing that a person being offered deliverance ministry has a diagnosis of a common mental disorder such as anxiety or depression, or a major mental illness such as schizophrenia, what should the medical advice be? Is deliverance precluded in such cases? Nor is it clear that absence of a current diagnosis necessarily means that deliverance ministry will be helpful, or even not harmful. The medical questions that arise are myriad, the published research base to guide answers is small, and the nature of good professional practice is likely – in most cases – to be very unclear.

Many lay people, including perhaps many clergy, are not aware of the differences between psychology and psychiatry and may not know which professional(s) to consult. In fact, a multidisciplinary mental health team is likely to include nurses, as well as psychiatrists and clinical psychologists, and may also include occupational therapists, social workers, and perhaps other psychotherapists or counsellors. In primary care, general practitioners, like all medical doctors, would have a basic level of training in psychiatry, but may or may not be equipped to deal with the complex issues that might arise in deliverance ministry. Similarly, not all psychologists are clinical psychologists and they may or may not have expertise relevant to the kinds of questions that arise in the course of deliverance ministry. General references to 'the resources of medicine' are therefore unhelpfully vague. In fact, the 1972 recommendation by the Exeter commission, that a referral be made to a 'physician in psychological medicine' (confusingly, this would be a psychiatrist – not a psychologist), is more specific and thus more helpful than much of the advice that has come afterwards.

The concept of diagnosis in psychiatry is not without its critics. Mental disorders (or 'mental illnesses') are often not associated with evidence of physical pathology (whether biochemical or anatomical) in the way that diagnoses are in other areas of medicine. Psychiatry is concerned with both mind and brain but, to a large extent, the application of the concept of diagnosis to disorders of mind is an analogy, or metaphor, based upon the medical model. Sometimes a psychiatric diagnosis can be harmful, conferring stigma and eliciting prejudice from others. However, a fundamental principle is that psychiatric diagnosis is based upon objective evidence of suffering and impaired ability to function effectively. Ideally, a diagnosis also predicts effective treatment(s) and likely prognosis. It is therefore of great practical importance and is one of the central concerns of psychiatry as the medical speciality devoted to the care of people suffering from mental disorders.

The relationships between psychiatry, possession states and deliverance ministry are complex, and a detailed discussion is beyond the scope of this brief essay. However, it is clear that beliefs concerning demon possession are to a large extent culturally determined and, even within a single religion such as Christianity, there are a range of theological views as to what constitutes demon possession or need for deliverance. Roland Littlewood, a psychiatrist and anthropologist, has suggested that (on a worldwide basis) demon possession is 'arguably the most common culture-bound psychiatric syndrome' (Littlewood 2004). Beliefs that one is 'possessed' may be completely normal in some contexts and need not be associated with a psychiatric diagnosis. On the other hand, Littlewood suggests, beliefs about demons and possession may provide popular explanations for what psychiatrists would diagnose as a mental disorder. In addition to this:

- the vocabulary of possession and deliverance may provide a way of trying to make sense of experiences that are difficult to verbalize
- the demonic may feature prominently in the psychopathology associated with mental illness
- people with diagnosed mental disorders may identify spiritual concerns (guilt, separation from God, fear of hell, etc.) that have not been adequately addressed within mental health services.

In addition to cultural anthropology, considerations of theological anthropology may be significant, particularly where doctors and clergy find themselves in conversation. There is no universally agreed concept of self across scientific disciplines, but most clinicians and scientists are wary of mind-body dualism and see the human being as a unitary entity. This approach is arguably consonant with Hebrew Scripture, which also has a unitary view of human beings. Of course, Western medical discourse does not see the human creature in relationship with God in the way that biblical authors did and is prone to a form of reductionism that is alien to Scripture. Problems arise, particularly in relation to certain readings of the New Testament, when the human being is understood to be vulnerable to discarnate spiritual entities that may be understood as the cause of physical or mental ailments. The apparent clash between scientific and theological accounts that results is amenable to resolution in various ways but, if not recognized, can lead to misunderstandings between clergy and medical professionals.

There is therefore scope for a wide range of possible conversations between a psychiatrist and a priest in respect of any particular person presented as a candidate for deliverance ministry. The two may agree (or collude) that someone is (or is not) possessed and in need of deliverance ministry or exorcism. They may both dismiss the ontological nature of demonic entities and resort to psychological or medical explanations. They may disagree, and perhaps retreat to professional silos, agreeing to disagree. Whatever the nature of the conversation, it is clear that both will be influenced by their theological views and expertise (or lack of it) as well as by their medical knowledge (or lack of it). Both, however, also have a professional obligation not to breach boundaries of competence and training, or to impose their views on those whom they seek to help clinically/pastorally.

A person with a mental illness is, by definition (within *The Safeguarding and Clergy Discipline Measure* 2016 and according to the Department of Health), a vulnerable person if that illness impairs their ability to protect themself from violence, abuse, neglect or exploitation. Both the medical professional and the priest involved in deliverance ministry thus have legal safeguarding obligations that need to be considered carefully in every case of deliverance ministry or exorcism.

Beliefs about possession and deliverance

While recognizing that deliverance may cover more than simply demon 'possession', it is helpful to recognize at the outset that the term 'possession' (or other related terms, such as demonic 'oppression', or 'demonization') denotes certain beliefs concerning the relationship between an individual and an alien spiritual force or entity. People may believe that they are possessed, or that others are possessed, for a variety of reasons. These beliefs may be based upon particular 'signs', or identifiable causes, and different churches and theological traditions have their own lists of these. They may include changed thoughts/ feelings, reaction to spiritual advice/objects, or experiences of feeling controlled by an alien will. For example, according to Michael Perry (1987, p. 120), signs of demonic oppression may include:

- indifference towards, or rejection of, God
- evil or anti-Christian thoughts
- habitual lying
- lack of remorse, inner restlessness, lack of peace
- negative reactions to Christian symbolism
- paranoid fears.

All of these may arise in the course of a mental illness and so it is very difficult – if these signs are considered in isolation – to know how 'normal' beliefs may be distinguished from psychopathology. A priest may consult a psychiatrist for further guidance but, equally, the psychiatrist would need to seek advice from the priest as to what expectations and beliefs were commonly accepted in relation to demon possession in that particular church. Beliefs are only 'normal', or unusual, within a personal, social and cultural context and diagnosis requires a good knowledge of the personal, spiritual and religious history, as well as wider cultural expectations. At risk of over-simplifying, beliefs about possession among mental health professionals (and I am focusing here on Christians – although I imagine that colleagues in other faith traditions may have similar debates) fall into three main groups:

1 The 'demonic' may operate as a metaphor or myth, and may be culturally and psychologically meaningful, but does not reflect any real entity in scientific terms. The task is therefore simply to diagnose the presence (or absence) of any underlying psychiatric disorder.

2 The demonic may be understood in a very literal (ontologically real) way and thus offers an alternative cause for mental phenomena. According to some who adopt this viewpoint, the psychiatrist

needs to make a differential diagnosis between mental illness and demonic influence (Sall 1976; Innamorati, et al. 2019). Alternatively, it may be proposed that demons cause mental illness (Irmak 2014).

3   Mental disorders and the demonic may be understood as operating in some way on different levels or dimensions, which may or may not mutually interact (Bufford 1989).

In Western medicine, the second of these viewpoints is less common, and more controversial (Karanci 2014), but not unheard of among medical professionals who belong to more conservative, or Charismatic, traditions.

Potential harms

The dangers here for abuse or neglect should by now be self-evident, but it is worth highlighting some of them more specifically:

- There may be a failure to diagnose a treatable mental disorder because psychopathology is misattributed to demonic influence.
- A mental disorder may be wrongly diagnosed through failure of a psychiatrist to understand the theological beliefs concerning demons within a particular congregation or church.
- A professional person (psychiatrist or priest) may easily be drawn into imposing their beliefs about possession/demons, etc., upon a vulnerable person in such a way as to adversely affect their mental wellbeing.
- Deliverance/exorcism may be psychologically harmful to a vulnerable person, whether or not they have a pre-existing psychiatric condition.
- A psychiatrist might experience a conflict of interests between their own spiritual/theological views and their responsibility for the mental health and wellbeing of a person receiving deliverance ministry.

Deliverance in Practice

There is anecdotal empirical evidence that exorcism/deliverance can sometimes be harmful in practice (Tajima-Pozo et al. 2011; Mercer 2013; Cook 2020, pp. 116–19). There is also evidence that it can sometimes be helpful (Maniam 1987) but, surprisingly, there seems never to have been a systematic follow-up study to delineate outcomes following exorcism or deliverance ministry. There is no clear definition of what constitutes deliverance ministry; liturgies for exorcism are not always publicly available, and practice varies. The psychiatrist advising a deliverance team is thus faced with the impossible task of advising on whether or not it is safe to administer a potentially harmful, and possibly undefined, psychological intervention[2] to a vulnerable person with no solid research evidence upon which to base their advice.

There has been particular concern about the impact of exorcism on patients with a diagnosis of dissociative identity disorder (DID; previously known as multiple personality disorder, MPD). In a study of 15 women with a diagnosis of MPD who believed, or had been told, that they were possessed, 14 had undergone exorcism (Bowman 1991). Exorcisms were traumatic for the majority of the women concerned and exacerbated dissociative symptoms. Thirteen reported that it was a painful/bad experience, and a similar number reported that it had had negative spiritual/religious impact upon them. Ten felt that they were coerced. In a study of seven patients with MPD who had been subjected to exorcism, the impact varied from mildly to severely negative, with adverse effects including exacerbation of the underlying condition, suicide attempts and reduced religious fervour (Fraser 1993). In a study of 47 separate exorcisms conducted on 15 patients with DID, Bull and colleagues (1998) reported that 24 gave completely positive evaluations of their experience of exorcism and 23 gave mixed responses. Those that gave positive evaluations were associated with a number of factors including, importantly, non-coercion.

Good psychiatric practice

As the specialty within medicine devoted to the diagnosis and treatment of mental disorder, psychiatry plays a potentially central role in managing deliverance ministry effectively and safely, to the benefit of the individual receiving ministry and their wider family, congregation and community. However, codes of good practice within psychiatry, and medicine more widely, do not make specific reference to deliverance ministry or exorcism.

Along with all doctors, the practice of psychiatrists within the UK is governed by the General Medical Council (GMC). In GMC guidance on *Personal Beliefs and Medical Practice* (General Medical Council 2013), it is made clear that patients should be treated fairly, whatever their choices and beliefs, and that a doctor should not express his/her personal beliefs (including religious beliefs) in ways that exploit patients' vulnerability, or cause distress. A patient's spiritual/religious concerns can legitimately be taken into account when making an assessment, but pressure should not be placed upon them to discuss or justify these beliefs. A doctor may only talk about their personal beliefs when asked by a patient to do so, or when they indicate that they would welcome such a discussion. Even then, the doctor's beliefs/values should not be imposed upon a patient.

The Royal College of Psychiatrists (RCPsych) provides more detailed guidance, relating the broader vision of *Good Medical Practice* offered by the GMC to the specific concerns of psychiatrists. Primarily this guidance is laid out within a document appropriately entitled *Good Psychiatric Practice*, but little is said there about spirituality/religion. In a Position Statement entitled *Recommendations for Psychiatrists on Spirituality and Religion* more specific guidance is provided (Cook 2013). This document does not say anything specifically about deliverance or exorcism. However, it makes recommendations concerning clinical assessment, psychiatric training, respect and sensitivity towards patients and colleagues, a prohibition against proselytizing, need for organizational policy and joint working with clergy/chaplains, all of which are relevant to the involvement of psychiatrists in deliverance ministry.

A variety of concerns arise for psychiatrists who might be called upon to work with a diocesan deliverance team in respect of any particular case. For example, some are wary of potential reputational damage that may be associated with such work. The person receiving deliverance ministry is highly likely to be another doctor's patient, raising questions about communication with colleagues and possible perceptions of interfering with the good medical practice of a colleague. In exceptional cases, the person receiving deliverance ministry may be assessed as requiring assessment under the Mental Health Act with a view to compulsory admission to hospital. Moreover, there are complex conceptual and diagnostic issues around exactly what demon possession is and how spiritual concerns relate to the biopsychosocial model that most doctors usually operate within. Most psychiatrists have not had a theological training and employ a different vocabulary to clergy when formulating their patients' problems and treatment plans.

Given this context, the question arises as to whether psychiatrists, or medical professionals in general, should ever be involved in deliverance ministry. It might be argued that there is too great a conflict of interests, and that a psychiatrist should never sanction, or appear to sanction, a potentially harmful intervention with no evidence base to guide when, whether, or in what circumstances it might be beneficial to a patient. On the other hand, deliverance ministry is primarily a spiritual intervention and – it might be argued – can be beneficial when administered with due safeguards. If psychiatrists (or other professionals competent to make a mental health assessment) were not to be involved, there would be no means of assessing whether or not a given person was mentally fit to undergo deliverance and the whole practice would effectively become impossible to administer safely.

Different considerations arise where the psychiatrist is already involved in clinical care of the patient (e.g. as the NHS consultant caring for the patient) as opposed to being invited by a deliverance team to participate as a third-party advisor. In the former case, the usual responsibilities of care apply, deliverance processes should be taken into account when making a clinical assessment and planning care, and local ethics mechanisms might need to be consulted. Obviously, nothing should be discussed with the deliverance team without the consent of the patient. The latter case is, however, somewhat more complicated.

What might good professional practice look like for psychiatrists who, outside of their usual clinical responsibilities for a patient, are consulted about, and/or invited to collaborate in, deliverance ministry? At this point, I am clearly expressing my own views, given that neither the GMC nor RCPsych has any approved policy or guidance on the topic. However, having discussed this with colleagues, and as a basis for further discussion, my proposed recommendations would be:

1   There needs to be a clear understanding of the role and accountability of the psychiatrist in the process, with their primary commitment being to the overall health and wellbeing of the person concerned. This should take into account spiritual as well as biological, psychological and social concerns but it needs to be clear that the psychiatrist's expertise is in mental health.

2   The psychiatrist should not be seen as actively facilitating, recommending, or participating in, deliverance ministry. (This would be the responsibility of others – e.g. the diocesan deliverance ministry team.)

3   The psychiatrist has a responsibility to show awareness of a range of Christian beliefs and to respect the beliefs of the person receiving ministry, even when they disagree with them.

4   A sensitive and respectful psychiatric assessment of the person receiving deliverance ministry should include a spiritual/religious history, past medical history (including mental health concerns)

and a careful mental state examination. The psychiatrist should not offer an opinion without seeing the person concerned.

5   Written consent should be obtained for gaining access to medical records, and discussions with responsible treating clinicians, where appropriate.

6   Deliverance ministry should never be coercive and should not involve imposition of views, values or beliefs upon the person receiving ministry. The psychiatrist should ensure that others have not placed pressure upon the person concerned to receive such ministry and should ensure that they are engaging with it on the basis of their own, freely made, choices and decisions. If there is any evidence of coercion, this becomes a safeguarding matter and the psychiatrist has an obligation to discuss this with the appropriate Diocesan Safeguarding Advisor (or other multi-agency safeguarding advisors, as appropriate).

7   A psychiatrist providing support to a deliverance ministry team needs to be aware of the potential harms of such ministry and do all that is possible to protect the person receiving ministry from these harms.

8   Collaboration with clergy, chaplains and lay ministers in the course of deliverance ministry needs to be approached with mutual respect and sensitivity, and with due regard to guidance offered by the church concerned (e.g. House of Bishops).

9   Assessment of the person concerned, advice offered and details of any other intervention, should be appropriately documented and discussed with a peer group, supervisor or mentor.

10   Involvement in deliverance ministry should be discussed during appraisal in support of revalidation with the GMC.

Should a psychiatrist be present during the exercise of deliverance ministry or exorcism? On the one hand, this might seem to be a wise precaution to protect a person from harm. On the other hand, it might be argued that this is not a medical procedure and that the psychiatrist would be subject to a conflict of interests. If requested to do so by the person concerned, I think a psychiatrist should be willing to respond positively and to be present as a professional advocate during the process. However, if present, the psychiatrist needs to be clear that their prime concern must be the wellbeing and safety of their patient, and that theological considerations take second place.

Indemnity

Medical practitioners in the UK are required by the GMC to have in place an appropriate medical indemnity policy. The GMC have powers to check that doctors are suitably insured, and to remove their licence to practice if they discover that they are not. While many relevant employers, including the NHS and some private healthcare providers, offer clinical negligence cover for doctors whom they employ, this does not cover work outside their contract of employment and most doctors therefore have personal indemnity cover to address these extra-contractual duties. The question arises as to whether or not involvement in deliverance ministry would be covered by the indemnity ordinarily held by most psychiatrists. Communications with providers of medical indemnity suggest that the probable answer is that it would not – unless specifically mentioned by the doctor when discussing cover required. Unfortunately, for reasons of confidentiality, no data is readily available concerning cases that may have been brought against doctors relating to their involvement in deliverance ministry.

Conclusion

Repeated guidance that mental health professionals should be involved in deliverance ministry and/or exorcism have failed to address the specifics of what is actually expected in practice. The lack of clarity concerning the nature of good practice, the potential for adverse outcomes, and the lack of a clear research evidence base present a worrying recipe for potential allegations of malpractice. Some proposed recommendations for good practice are offered as a basis for further debate.

References

The Archbishops' Commission, 1958, *The Church's Ministry of Healing*, London: Church Information Board.

Elizabeth S. Bowman, 1991, 'Clinical and Spiritual Effects of Exorcism in Fifteen Patients with Multiple Personality Disorder', *Dissociation* VI, pp. 222–38.

Rodger K. Bufford, 1989, 'Demonic Influence and Mental Disorders', *Journal of Psychology and Christianity* 8, pp. 35–48.

Dennis L. Bull, Joan W. Ellason and Colin A. Ross, 1998, 'Exorcism Revisited: Positive Outcomes with Dissociative Identity Disorder', *Journal of Psychology and Theology* 26, 188–96.

Christopher C. H. Cook, 2013, *Recommendations for Psychiatrists on Spirituality and Religion*, London: Royal College of Psychiatrists.

Christopher C. H. Cook, 2020, *Christians Hearing Voices: Affirming Experience and Finding Meaning*, London: Jessica Kingsley.

George A. Fraser, 1993, 'Exorcism Rituals: Effects on Multiple Personality Disorder Patients', *Dissociation* VI, pp. 239–44.

General Medical Council, 2013, *Personal Beliefs and Medical Practice*, London: General Medical Council.

A. S. Hale and N. R. Pinninti, 1994, 'Exorcism-Resistant Ghost Possession Treated with Clopenthixol', *British Journal of Psychiatry* 165, pp. 386–8.

Marco Innamorati, Ruggero Taradel and Renato Foschi, 2019 'Between Sacred and Profane: Possession, Psychopathology, and the Catholic Church', *History of Psychology* 22.1, pp. 1–16.

M. Kemal Irmak, 2014, 'Schizophrenia or Possession?', *Journal of Religion and Health* 53, pp. 773–7.

A. Nuray Karanci, 2014, 'Concerns About Schizophrenia or Possession?' *Journal of Religion and Health* 53, pp. 1691–2.

Roland Littlewood, 2004, 'Possession States', *Psychiatry* 3, pp. 8–10.

T. Maniam, 1987, 'Exorcism and Psychiatric Illness: Two Case Reports', *The Medical Journal of Malaysia* 42, pp. 317–19.

Jean Mercer, 2013, 'Deliverance, Demonic Possession, and Mental Illness: Some Considerations for Mental Health Professionals', *Mental Health, Religion & Culture* 16, pp. 595–611.

Michael Perry (ed.), 1987, *Deliverance: Psychic Disturbances and Occult Involvement*, London: SPCK.

Dom Robert Petitpierre (ed.), 1972, *Exorcism: The Report of a Commission Convened by the Bishop of Exeter*, London: SPCK.

Millard J. Sall, 1976, 'Demon Possession or Psychopathology?: A Clinical Differentiation', *Journal of Psychology and Theology* 4, pp. 286–90.

Kazuhiro Tajima-Pozo, Diana Zambrano-Enriquez, Laura de Anta, et al., 2011, 'Practicing Exorcism in Schizophrenia', *BMJ Case Report*, bcr1020092350.

F. D. Whitwell and M. G. Barker, 1980, '"Possession" in Psychiatric Patients in Britain', *British Journal of Medical Psychology* 53, pp. 287–95.

Working Party on Healing, 2000, *A Time to Heal: A Contribution Towards the Ministry of Healing*, London: Church House Publishing.

P. M. Yap, 1960, 'The Possession Syndrome: A Comparison of Hong Kong and French Findings', *Journal of Mental Science* 106, pp. 114–37.

Francis Young, 2018, *A History of Anglican Exorcism: Deliverance and Demonology in Church Ritual*, London: I.B. Tauris.

Notes

1 https://www.churchofengland.org/safeguarding/safeguarding-e-manual/safeguarding-children-young-people-and-vulnerable-adults/4-1 (accessed 6.2.24).

2 I recognize that, from a certain Christian point of view, the intervention is primarily a spiritual one. However, it is also a psychological

one, and the spiritual and psychological aspects cannot be disentangled. As a professional in psychological medicine, it is the primary responsibility of the psychiatrist to consider the psychological impact of the intervention.

PART 2

Theologies and Cultures

5

Deliverance From Evil:
Exorcism in the Lord's Prayer

Matthias Grebe

Introduction

In his monograph, *The Defeat of Satan: Karl Barth's Three-Agent Account of Salvation*, Declan Kelly writes:

> In John's first epistle, the apostle declares to his readers the purpose behind the Son of God's coming: "to destroy the works of the devil" (1 John 3.8). Modern theology has had a complicated relationship with New Testament declarations of this kind. Are these idiosyncratic descriptions of the Christian understanding of salvation inhabiting the margins of New Testament thought? Do they reflect merely one of several discrete metaphors – one that is neither more nor less important than the others – used by the scriptural authors to convey the meaning of the atonement? Or do they in fact take us to the very heart of the gospel, summing up in a few words the biblical doctrine of salvation? (Kelly 2022, p. 1)

After a short outline of the reception history of 'evil' in post-enlightenment Christian dogmatics, the first part of this chapter will look at the Russian Orthodox theologian Sergius Bulgakov and the German-American Protestant theologian Paul Tillich, who complement each others' work on the ontology of being and non-being. The second part will focus on prayer, in particular the final petition of the Lord's Prayer, before offering some concluding thoughts. The central question addressed here is 'what do we mean when we pray "Deliver us from evil"?'

'Evil' in the post-enlightenment era

The work of Friedrich Schleiermacher in the first half of the nineteenth century, and in particular his work on salvation, advanced a 'Theology without Satan',[1] which was later bolstered by Albrecht Ritschl's influential work on the doctrine of salvation (see Ritschl 1872; Ritschl 1902). Schleiermacher 'finds no substantial New Testament evidence for the notion that Satan is a real "overlord" of humanity and that the coming of the Son of God was intended to break the power of the devil' (Schleiermacher 1999, pp. 165–6). Schleiermacher's concern is that a view of humanity as in Satan's grip 'gravely strengthens the already strong inclination of men to deny their *own* guilt' (pp. 168; emphasis added). Instead, he advocates an increased concentration on 'our own inner life', something he sees stressed in Scripture. Schleiermacher saw no future for the devil in dogmatic work and anticipated that the notion of the devil would eventually become 'obsolete' (p. 168).

However, in the middle of the twentieth century, Paul Althaus declared that 'the age of a theology without Satan has come to an end' (1962, p. 391). Without effecting a complete return to the traditional view of the devil, Karl Barth in his monumental *Church Dogmatics* did much to 'refute the assumption that a "theology without Satan" was the only reasonable option for a discourse desiring to be taken seriously as a science' (Kelly 2022, p. 2), though there did remain in his work a certain unwillingness to 'elevate the position of Satan within the dogmatic task' (p. 4). Barth writes that 'It is nonsense to talk about God and the devil … in the same breath' (Barth 1956–75, Vol. 3, p. 520). He therefore cautions his readers that we should think and speak of the devil 'only reluctantly, infrequently, and with great reserve' (p. 261).

I share some of Schleiermacher's pastoral and ethical concerns, and his desire not simply to adopt the devil as a 'scapegoat', but instead take responsibility for one's own sin, retaining the Christian practice of 'severe self-examination' (Schleiermacher 1999, p. 169).[2] I also agree with Barth's reluctance to speak about evil as a personified entity. However, questions remain about the role that 'evil' plays in our theological work more broadly, about what we actually mean by evil, and about why it is included in our liturgies and prayers. So before we answer the central question, 'what do we mean when we pray "Deliver us from evil"?', let us first look at the nature of evil itself.

Evil as privation

'Does evil *exist* as an independent principle of being, as a "substance," alongside good?' (Bulgakov 2002, p. 147). As Bulgakov points out, the 'philosophers of antiquity, the church fathers, and the scholastic theologians all unanimously answered this question in the negative: evil does *not exist* alongside good as an independent principle, a principle that competes with and is parallel to good' (p. 147). For Bulgakov, evil is 'not a substance but a *state* of creaturely being' and the 'absence of good, *sterēsis*, *privatio*, an accident, a parasite of being' (p. 147). Christianity is not a dualistic religion, of two equal and opposing principles, so any framework advocating a good god and an evil god or the dualism of light versus darkness or matter versus the spiritual must be seen as 'completely incompatible' with the teaching and beliefs of the Church (p. 147). As Ford stresses, that which is sometimes called John's 'dualism' 'never takes for granted that God's love for the world is completely successful in getting its desired response' (Ford 2021, p. 132). The 'Evil One' that the New Testament speaks of, e.g. in the Gospel of John, is a rebellious *creature* rather than some kind of equal and opposing evil *force* threatening the loving nature of the creator God.

Put differently, and ontologically speaking then, 'only Good, only

God and His power in creation exists … [and] evil does not exist, but is a phantom of nonbeing' (Bulgakov 2002, p. 147). Or as Barth put it, evil is *nothingness*, a 'fleeting shadow' (Barth 1956–75, Vol. 3, pp. 352, 361), it is defeated and accompanies the light of Jesus Christ only as God's rejection (Vol. 2, p. 122), that which God does not will [*Unwille*] (Vol. 3, pp. 353, 355, 360, 361, 363).

However, in light of the destructive force of evil in the world, is it sufficient to expose evil simply as an ontological *nothingness*? Because that would beg the question as to why Jesus included it in the seventh and final petition of the Prayer that he taught to his disciples.

What then is evil? How, if God did not create it, did it come into the world – where did it come from? And if, as Bulgakov says, evil is not a substance but a '*state* of being', how did this state become possible?

This chapter does not allow for a detailed exposition of all this, but evil does not exist in the divine life – only in the created world as a 'parasite'. There is a certain precondition in the nature of creatures and the world that allows 'space' *for* evil which, in itself, is not (yet) evil but nevertheless provides the possibility for it.[3] This 'precondition' might best be described as the separation of *potentiality* and *actuality* in the creaturely realm. Whereas God is infinite freedom and in God is fullness (God is *actus purus*, i.e. God is fully actual), creatures have finite freedom *for* God (and *for* the other) (see Bonhoeffer 1997, pp. 60–7), in whom this fullness (i.e. God's plan and purpose for creation) needs to be *actualized* (see Tillich 1967, Vol. 2, p. 31). Every part of being 'belongs *to the all* without actually being *in the all*' (Bulgakov 2002, p. 148). Humans are composites of essence and existence, beings who have potentiality of self-realization that is not actualized (p. 148).[4] This state of *limitedness*, innate to all finite (i.e. created and therefore contingent) beings, coupled with creaturely-finite *freedom* bestowed by the Creator, allows for the process of *becoming* in the creaturely realm (i.e. potential, possibilities and ideas can be actualized). The flipside of creaturely life is that 'its fragmented or partial character also signifies that it is not infallible' (p. 148), as humans can make positive (life-enhancing) or negative (life-destroying) choices with their given freedom. As Bulgakov, echoing Paul in 1 Corinthians 15.28, writes: 'This state exists as long as there is no fullness, as long as God is not in the all and the all is not in God' (p. 148).

Furthermore, perfection is not given to the creaturely realm, but something humans seek by actualizing creaturely *creativity* (see Phil. 3.12; Eph. 4.13; 1 John 2.5). This is 'synonymous with life' and God's path for humans (Bulgakov 2002, p. 149), a creaturely existence in the process of *becoming* (creation is not a *perpetuum mobile*) (p. 148–50). Without such freedom, creativity and autonomy, creation would be dead. Its task is to actualize itself and ascend on the path of virtue, from imperfection to the state of perfection, in which God will be all in all. Thus, the lack of perfection, an imperfection in all created beings on earth as well as in heaven, is therefore not simply due to sin, but part of the non-infallible state of creatureliness, which is part of God's plan to perfect this world. To summarize: 'The creative self-determination of creatures is subject to imperfection and error, allows for different paths and possibilities. But imperfection and the presence of different possibilities are not yet evil, just as error is not sin. Rather, they simply characterize becoming as such' (p. 148). The possibility – or rather inevitability – of errors in nature, which are not yet evil, nevertheless creates 'space' for evil.

Evil in the world

How then is evil actualized? As we have seen, the world 'out of nothing' is created on the basis of freedom and creaturely self-determination. Here the picture of light and darkness is a helpful biblical analogy: 'God is light, and in him is no darkness at all' (1 John 1.5). The light of God shines into the darkness of the human world and the human heart. In creation, God dispels the darkness, the *nothing*, the abyss, the *nihil* out of which we are created. Yet the boundary of *nothing* remains a passive resistance in this world. And this means that creaturely life and (relative) freedom operate not in a vacuum, but as connected to two paths or possibilities within time, with two opposing principles of good and evil, heading to two opposed ontological poles, being and non-being. We can think in terms of two paths, one of light and life towards perfection and deification, of holiness, grateful obedience, conformity and acceptance of God's Lordship, and (conscious) dependence on God, and another path of darkness and death towards *nothing*, one of disobedience, arbitrariness, caprice and (illusionary) independence to the divine will, which Dostoevsky called 'living by one's own dumb will' and which will eventually end in nothing. Whereas the first path is characterized by a deep abundance of abiding joy and peace, the second is one of fear and anxiety, caused by the constant threat of nonbeing.

Yet, as Tillich writes, 'being is essentially related to nonbeing' (1967, p. 202). This chiaroscuro of being in the world, this combination and togetherness of light and shadow 'reflects the changing character of creaturely life' (Bulgakov 2002, p. 156). Whereas divine fullness and divine love and light are unchanging, human love is characterized by increase and decrease (p. 156). In this world, and in time, good and evil *arise* together in us.

Evil is actualized when the human heart (which is where the possibility of evil nestles) is tempted from the outside, yet from within the created world, and this misdirected human desire is acted upon.[5] Paul Tillich describes this process of 'awakening',[6] as a *transition* from essential being (1967, Vol. 2, p. 33) a state of 'non-actualized potentiality' or 'dreaming innocence' (p. 62), to existence.[7] Tillich writes that 'The state of dreaming innocence drives beyond itself. The possibility of the transition to existence is experienced as temptation.'[8] The outcome of this state of existence is what he calls *estrangement* (p. 44ff.). A person is 'estranged from the ground of his being [God], from other beings, and from himself' (p. 44), and this is expressed in unbelief, hubris and concupiscence and contradicts a person's essential being and potential for goodness (p. 59). This self-contradiction ultimately drives humanity toward self-destruction and thus evil, which is a weakening of the love for God, is created by creatures and their own self-wilfulness (see Bulgakov 2002, p. 164). It is actualized when the first path of light is disrupted and a path for darkness is opened by creaturely freedom, self-determination or self-realization, and creativity *against* God's will. Ultimately, evil is 'rebellion against God and hostility toward Him' (p. 153), a path of deception (Gen. 3) and self-deception that traps humanity (p. 161–2) as in the end, evil is 'self-destruction' (Tillich 1967, Vol. 2, p. 202), a 'spiritual self-enslavement of creatures, their enslavement by their own nature ... under the masks or pretend genius of self-deification' (Bulgakov 2002, p. 155).

The Lord's Prayer and exorcism

Turning to the Lord's Prayer, Luther's picture of the person *incurvatus in se* is helpful here. When we look only at ourselves, all we see is darkness and act accordingly. Rather than gazing downwards into our human abyss, we need to look upwards to the light of Christ, who has conquered evil on the cross and in whom all things on earth and heaven are joined together into unity (Col. 1; Eph. 1).[9] In order to be delivered from evil, we need to cleave to God. So how do we cleave to God? In prayer! Prayer is not something we *do* or initiate. Rather 'prayer is God' and God is prayer, God's indwelling (see Ware 1986, p. 2). So prayer is something we share in – the divine life – something God is doing in us (p. 3). It is a re-orientation of our estranged lives towards the divine light that shines in the darkness. In prayer, we humble ourselves before the wisdom and omnipotence of God and acknowledge his Lordship over this world and our lives. Through God's loving embrace in prayer, the Spirit gives us the courage to face our own sinfulness without fear of condemnation, as well as the power to ascend on the path of virtue from imperfection to the state of perfection (the ascent of our desires to seek God alone), knowing that Christ has overcome the 'threat of nonbeing' and has died to set us free (see Tillich 1967, Vol. 1, pp. 64, 110, 195, 209, 273). 'Deliver us from Evil' is thus the cry of someone who is aware of this struggle of good and evil in the world (Romans 7) and of Christ's victory over sin, death and the devil. The deliverance sought in the Lord's Prayer is the throwing of oneself into the loving and saving embrace of God, who is our protection and deliverer in times of sorrow, need and temptation, and who empowers us to live in freedom as children of God.

In our liturgies, the Lord's Prayer needs to be seen as part of the wider Christian walk, and the minor act of exorcism that takes place when we collectively pray the final petition should be understood as rooted in the sacraments. Kallistos Ware writes that 'the name of Jesus has power' and the 'Invocation of the divine Name possesses a sacramental character, serving as an efficacious sign of his invisible presence and action' (1986, p. 11). As St Gregory of Sinai maintains, 'Prayer is the manifestation of Baptism' (p. 2). 'The aim of the Christian life is to return to the perfect grace of the Holy and Life-giving Spirit, which was conferred upon us at the beginning in divine Baptism' (p. 3). True prayer signifies the 'rediscovery and "manifestation" of our baptismal grace' (p. 3). The purpose of the final petition of the Lord's prayer can be summarized as 'become what you are … become consciously and actively, what you already are potentially and secretly, by virtue of your creation according to your divine image and your re-reaction in Baptism' (p. 3).

Exorcism, from the Greek *exorkismós*, a rite of expulsion, literally 'binding by oath', takes place in baptism, when Christ *claims* us for his own or *binds* us to himself, by receiving the sign of his cross.

As in baptism, when the candidate receives the sign of the cross and is asked to reject the spiritual forces and evil powers of this world, praying the Lord's Prayer also represents a similar minor act of exorcism. This does not necessarily denote demonic possession and the casting out of evil spirits but, as with the signing of the cross at baptism, invoking or calling upon the name of the Lord in times of temptation has power, derived from the cross of Christ and 'utterly [destroying] all that is evil' (Ware 1986, p. 11).

Exorcism has as much to do with 'closing doors' – i.e. being *sealed* by the power of the Holy Spirit – as it does with casting out evil thoughts and renewing our minds towards God. When we pray the Lord's Prayer then, it is therefore not simply a self-exorcism we practise, not only an act of mindfulness, but a divine act of exorcism by the power of the Holy Spirit, the divine light.

It therefore matters very little whether the Greek word for 'evil' – πονηρός (*poneros*) – is rendered as 'evil' in general or 'the Evil one' (as the *Didache* indicates the early Church prayed), as both interpretations come to the same thing as Hauerwas (1996) writes:

> The power of evil must be admitted and taken seriously, yet not too seriously. Perhaps that is why, though the Lord's Prayer honestly focuses upon trial, temptation and evil, it never mentions Satan by name. Evil is a threatening power, though a defeated one. Though the battle rages, we know who has won the war (p. 94).

Conclusion

In conclusion, let us turn again to our initial question – 'what do we mean when we pray "Deliver us from evil"?' The deliverance we require and for which we pray with the Lord's Prayer is not only or even primarily attributed to adverse situations, but to the very possibility of evil that resides within our hearts. As Hauerwas highlights, when we pray for deliverance from evil, we acknowledge: 1) 'that we have not the resources, on our own, to resist evil'; and 2) 'that God is greater than any foe of God' (1996, p. 94). The Litany in the *Book of Common Prayer*, which we pray after Morning Prayer on Sundays, Wednesdays and Fridays, makes the somewhat abstract 'evil' of the Lord's Prayer utterly concrete. It spells it out:

From all evil and mischief; from sin, from the crafts and assaults of the devil; from thy wrath, and from everlasting damnation ... From all blindness of heart; from pride, vain-glory and hypocrisy; from envy, hatred and malice, and all uncharitableness ... From fornication, and all other deadly sin; from all the deceits of the world, the flesh, and the devil ... From all sedition, privy conspiracy and rebellion; from all false doctrine, heresy and schism; from hardness of heart and contempt of thy Word and Commandment, *Good Lord, deliver us.*

The basis for victory over evil in everyday life is 'found in the sacraments – in baptism and in the celebration of the Eucharist' and in 'continuous prayer in faith, as expressed in the seventh and final petition of the Lord's Prayer: "deliver us from evil"' (Grebe 2017, p. 711), a prayer that acknowledges that we have to turn from 'darkness to light and from the power of Satan to God' (Acts 26.18). Thus, by praying the *first* petitions, we frame the evil in our own thoughts and actions in the light of God and in the *final* petition we pray to be set free from it, rededicating ourselves to a renewed service of God, so that God may be all in all.

References

Paul Althaus, 1962, *Die christliche Wahrheit: Lehrbuch der Dogmatik*, Gütersloh: Gütersloher Verlagshaus.

Karl Barth, 1956–75, *Church Dogmatics*, trans. G. W. Bromiley and T. F. Torrance, 4 vols, Edinburgh: T&T Clark.

Dietrich Bonhoeffer, 1997, *Creation and Fall: A Theological Exposition of Genesis 1–3*, Dietrich Bonhoeffer Works, Vol. 3, ed. John W. de Gruchy, trans. Douglas S. Bax, Minneapolis: Fortress Press.

Sergius Bulgakov, 2002, *The Bride of the Lamb*, trans. Boris Jakim, Edinburgh: T&T Clark.

Issak A. Dorner, 1882, *A System of Christian Doctrine*, Vol. 3, trans. Alfred Cave and J. S. Banks, Edinburgh: T&T Clark.

David F. Ford, 2021, *The Gospel of John: A Theological Commentary*, Grand Rapids: Baker Academic.

Matthias Grebe, 2017, 'The Problem of Evil', in Adam J. Johnson (ed.), *T&T Clark Companion to Atonement*, London: Bloomsbury T&T Clark, pp.707–12.

Stanley Hauerwas and H. William Willimon, 1996, *Lord, Teach Us: The Lord's Prayer & the Christian Life*, Nashville: Abingdon Press.

Declan Kelly, 2022, *The Defeat of Satan: Karl Barth's Three-Agent Account of Salvation Defeat of Satan*, London: T&T Clark.

Albrecht Ritschl, 1872, *A Critical History of the Christian Doctrine of Justification and Reconciliation*, trans. John S. Black, Edinburgh: Edmonston and Douglas.

Albrecht Ritschl, 1902, *The Christian Doctrine of Justification and Reconciliation*, ed. H. R. Mackintosh and A. B. Macaulay, Edinburgh: T&T Clark.

Friedrich D. E. Schleiermacher, 1999, *The Christian Faith*, ed. H. R. Mackintosh and J. S. Stewart, London: T&T Clark.

Paul Tillich, 1967, *Systematic Theology*, Chicago: The University of Chicago Press.

Kallistos Ware, 1986, *The Power of the Name: The Jesus Prayer in Orthodox Spirituality*, Oxford: SLG Press.

Notes

1 Isaak Dorner describes Schleiermacher as 'the most acute opponent of the doctrine of the devil' (1882, pp. 94–5).

2 This essay focuses on ethical, responsible living and *external* human action and the transformation towards fullness and *freedom* – a person's gradual acquisition of divine characteristics and virtues that reflect God's perfection. However, there is also an *internal* transformation taking place, one of purification and sanctification of our being, and an inward transformation marked by growth in *holiness*. Both the external and the internal transformation is rooted in the Christ-event and the

forgiveness of sins. Christ, the image of God, restores humanity, as Christ is the first fruit of the new creation in whom being (holiness) and action (freedom) are in complete harmony; *perfect holiness* (see 2 Cor. 7.1). By participating in the Christ-event through the sacraments, a person is incorporated into union with Christ by the Holy Spirit to share in the triune life.

3 For a more detailed analysis see Bulgakov, pp.148–64 (chapter on 'Evil').

4 Tillich writes that being a creative means both to be rooted in the creative ground of the divine life and to actualize oneself through freedom. Creation is fulfilled in the creaturely self-realization that simultaneously is freedom and destiny. But it is fulfilled through separation from the creative ground through a break between existence and essence.

5 As Bulgakov writes, 'The history of fallen humanity has a prologue in heaven, and evil in a pure form (and not as a fruit of ignorance, misunderstanding, deception, and self-deception) first appears in the spiritual world' (p. 160).

6 See Bulgakov, who writes 'By contrast, in man the knowledge of evil also became the beginning of the introduction of good, a new, special awakening of the principle that constitutes the positive essence of man's being' (p. 163).

7 'Adam must be understood as essential man and as symbolizing the transition from essence to existence' (Tillich, Vol. 2, p. 56). See also Tillich, Vol. 1, p. 205 and Vol. 2, pp. 29–44.

8 'Temptation is unavoidable because the state of dreaming innocence is uncontested and undecided' (Tillich, Vol. 2, p. 34).

9 'Our spiritual strategy should be positive and not negative: instead of trying to empty our mind of what is evil, we should fill it with the thought that is good' (Ware 1986, p. 13).

6

Brief and Inexpensive:
Exorcism in a London Pentecostal Community

Nicholas Adams

The practice of deliverance in the Church of England presents a possibility for providing pastoral care under difficult circumstances. The purpose of this brief chapter is to test three proposals. The first is that the extensive experience of diaspora communities with deliverance ministry is a valuable resource for Church traditions who are newer to the practice. The second is that the languages used in diaspora communities to describe deliverance are often low-key and close to the language of everyday life: they are not particularly out of the ordinary. The third is that practices of deliverance should provoke curiosity from those who engage them because their meaning is not self-evident. To elaborate these proposals I draw extensively on the work of the linguistic anthropologist Kirsty Rowan (Rowan 2016).

At the end of the 1900s, the English anthropologist Timothy Jenkins published *Religion in English Everyday Life* (Jenkins 1999). It attracted intense interest because of several odd and intriguing features. It was an account of some fieldwork done in a suburban town near Bristol: it was located in a particular place and offered a lot of detail about it. The word 'religion' does not actually appear as a guiding category in the study at all; instead, the focus is on practices of various kinds. And it made the bold claim that what are often named 'religious' practices are best interpreted as ways of making sense of the world and adapting to changing circumstances.

The connection with discussions about deliverance may not be immediately obvious, but I would argue it has to do with how one pays attention to things. Jenkins' most arresting claim is this: the everyday practices of life in small towns often seems banal to city-dwelling theorists. What small town folk do often seems inconsequential and devoid of interest. It is for this reason that urban-based anthropologists prefer to do fieldwork in more exciting places where more unusual (to city-dwellers, that is) affairs are afoot. Jenkins issues a warning: do not be misled by what appears to be banal. One needs to learn to use the local categories, the concepts and ideas of the practitioners. More colloquially: just because it would be banal if *you* were to do it, with *your* own reasons, that does not mean it is banal in any stronger sense. And to put it very pointedly: if you take something to be banal and uninteresting, that may be a sign that you need to learn new categories, and to acquire a deeper familiarity with the lives of those whose practices you dismiss.

I intend to apply this excellent advice to the opposite problem. We have gathered this collection of essays because something is happening in our communities that is the opposite of banal. The rise of deliverance ministry is not banal at all: it is *interesting*. Not only interesting: it appears exotic, fascinating and compelling. Jesus in the Gospels from time to time does battles with demons, but for decades – in the wake of historical-critical scholarship of the Bible – this was explained away as an artefact of the *mentalité* of the ancient world, a husk to be pried away from the kernel of the *kerygma*, a reflection of a worldview that no modern person would or could hold. But now, on our doorsteps, there are communities, often African diaspora communities, regularly doing battle with demons. This brings long-dormant aspects of the Gospel vividly back to life and offers an opportunity to embrace a much more literal reading of the demon passages: Mark 1.21, 3.20, 5.1, 7.24, 9.14; Matthew 8.28, 12.22, 15.21, 17.14; Luke 4.31, 4.41, 8.26, 9.37, 11.14. Out with the new, in with the old.

Deliverance ministry thus runs the risk of becoming another casualty of the culture wars. One's position with respect to exorcism becomes a marker for where one stands in the battle between conservatives and liberals, between plain sense and pragmatic senses of Scripture (often cast as literal vs figurative). If fighting demons becomes a proxy for fighting liberals, that will be a deep disappointment. It will place vulnerable people at risk. It will also be a profound disservice to those communities for whom deliverance ministry is an ordinary part of liturgical life.

I do want to draw attention to a tendency to see deliverance ministry in general, and exorcism of demons in particular, as especially interesting and exciting. I do think it is interesting, for reasons that will emerge in due course. But I want to suggest that just as for Timothy Jenkins the religious practices of small English towns are not banal, so for Kirsty Rowan the practices of diaspora communities are not exotic. If we find them exotic then – to adapt Jenkins' advice to anthropologists – this may be a sign that we need to learn new categories, and to acquire a deeper familiarity with the communities who practise deliverance ministry.

The linguist Kirsty Rowan produced in 2016 a report: '"Who are you in this body?": Identifying demons and the path to deliverance in a London Pentecostal Church'. It was the outcome of fieldwork in a London Pentecostal community in November 2013.

It is a quick matter to rehearse the facts. The community had rented a 1,200 capacity theatre in the East End of London and pretty much filled it. This Nigerian diaspora community were linked to the home community via a live televised link. It was quite a long period of worship which incorporated deliverance ministry, which took place rather later on in the proceedings. Here is Rowan's account directly:

> Late in the afternoon, once sermons, talks, music, singing and prayers have been performed and conducted, the London church

is addressed from Nigeria by the 'prophet' of this church by a live televised link that is also streamed on the web. The 'prophet' informs the audience that he has specially sent blessed water to be sprayed on the congregants by the evangelists in London. It is after this address and the 'prophet's' prayer that many members of the audience start to exhibit agitated forms of behaviour, which can be categorized as indexes of possession (Haustein 2011), such as vomiting, crying, falling to the floor, shaking and convulsing. The evangelists' attendants bring these individuals to the front of the theatre, but not onto the stage, and position them in a horizontal line. Other congregants who did not display this behaviour are invited to also join the 'prayer line' to receive the blessed water.

Starting at the beginning of the prayer line, the five evangelists take turns in dispensing the blessed water by spraying the participants in the face. The evangelists all have microphones and proceed to question one-by-one only those participants of the prayer line who recoil or react to being sprayed with the water. The attendants act as minders to assist with the physical safety of participants and the evangelists. The evangelists confirm the possession and perform the deliverance within a couple of minutes. Given the number of participants who join the deliverance prayer line, the evangelists must precipitate this ritual to allow all demon-possessed participants to be delivered within a prescribed timeframe. (pp. 250–1)

Rowan's professional interest is linguistic. So the detail of her analysis has as its focus the language used in the exorcism. She is particularly interested in the linguistic practices of both 'evangelists' and 'participants', and pays attention to questions of intonation, vocabulary and structure – especially the fact that the evangelists follow a routine, a script, in which the same four questions are typically addressed to the demons: 'who are you?', 'what have you done to this woman?', 'how long have you been there?' and 'how did you get in to her body?' Once these questions have been answered, the demon is commanded to leave, in the name of Jesus and with the anointing water.

Rowan is also interested in rhythm: the evangelist speaks, and the woman (the participants are nearly all women) responds. For the most part, in response to 'Who are you?' the demons are named as Anger, Depression, Lust, Death and so forth (p. 265). These are the demons who blight the lives of the women who present themselves for exorcism, and they overlap significantly with what in earlier times were called the seven deadly sins.

With a noticeable economy of means, the demons announce themselves, declare their activity, and are dismissed by the evangelist. But not in every case. The implicit rule governing question and answer is proved by an exception: the case of the participant named Anna, who is not familiar with the deliverance practices. Anna is in fact first in line for exorcism, but her case is presented by Rowan last because it is anomalous. Because Anna is first in line, and because she is inexperienced, she does not know what to do. She does not have a chance to observe others, and so she does the best she can. Anna talks over the evangelist – she does not wait for him to ask his questions – and does not answer his questions satisfactorily. The rhythm is disrupted. Instead of answering who the demon is, and instead of answering the question about what the demon has done, Anna's demon repeatedly tells the evangelist to go away. Whereas for other participants the demons obediently identify themselves, Anna's demon remains unnamed. Somewhat exasperated, or perhaps fatigued, the evangelist cuts short the process. He does not ask how long or how the demon got there. Instead he abruptly declares the woman clean, in Jesus' name, and Anna has to move aside for the next in line.

My interest is less in the linguistic details – fascinating though they are, and presented with exceptional clarity in the report – and more in certain features that her report notes but does not highlight. I wish to highlight them.

In Rowan's report, and in a companion piece published around the same time, jointly authored with Karen Dwyer (who has an interest in the linguistics of psychopathologies), Rowan makes several crucial observations that are important for our purposes (Rowan and Dwyer 2015). They are somewhat underplayed in her report, and my role is here is to amplify them so that their significance can be more clearly seen.

First, the service is well publicized on the web in advance, but no mention is made of deliverance ministry. It is not an advertised feature.

Second, no charge is made for attendance: it is free to attend (and there are over 1,000 attendees).

Third, it is a brisk matter. Each deliverance lasts two to three minutes.

Rowan has an hour and 20 minutes of video of the deliverance portion, but a significant portion of this time is devoted, at the start, to identifying who needs deliverance. There are three phases to this identification. The initial phase is a signal for candidates to start swaying or convulsing. Next, the attendants identify these person: those who display these signs, and several others, are brought to the front. There is quite a number of people in a horizontal row.

Finally, the five evangelists spray water in their faces. Those who react strongly are selected for deliverance: on this occasion there are 17. It is a quick and efficient process of selection. The crucial thing to notice is the brevity of the exorcism itself. Although the selection process takes a little time, each exorcism takes around two minutes. That is certainly longer than administering individual communion, but to those whose ideas of exorcism derive from novels, plays and movies this must appear arrestingly brief.

Fourth, the deliverance ministry is an ordinary practice with clear expectations for participants. The evangelists, the participants and the demons for the most part know their roles and for the most part play them fluently. Everyone gets in line, knows what to do, and gets on with it. The anomaly case 'Anna' shows not only what the norms are, but the pragmatism of the exorcist in cutting things short, and getting through the line.

These four features are interesting, although hardly exotic. They can be summarized. Deliverance is not advertised, it is free, it is fast, and it (mostly) has a simple repeated structure of questions, answers and deliverance.

Its efficiency is particularly noteworthy. There are nearly 1,200 people in attendance. This is whittled down to 17 deliverances in around 15 minutes through the expert diagnostic use of blessed water, and then a further 40–50 mins or so to carry out 17 deliverances.

What might we make of this?

This is a diaspora community from Nigeria within travelling distance of East London. The practice of deliverance is obviously a normal part of their worship. It does not even need to be advertised: everyone knows what to do and when to do it. It is an ordinary, everyday practice. The existence of demons is no big issue. Indeed it is not an issue at all: it is simply presupposed, in the same way that members of Western societies have since the late nineteenth century presupposed the existence of germs (displacing miasma as the supposed cause of disease). Like germs, demons are a serious but manageable threat to the community and to the lives of those afflicted by them. They are quickly named, their ill effects are quickly identified, and they are quickly dispatched, restoring agency to the individual, and restoring the individual, now healed, to the community.

Diaspora communities adapt to changing circumstances in various ways: this hybrid event (in person and online) is one of many available resources and, in the case of the event documented by Rowan, the presenting issue seems often to be women's difficulties with relationships, especially around questions of virtue and control. The purpose of the exorcism is in part to displace guilt, to restore women's reputations and to reassert women's agency. It does this quickly and efficiently.

To circle back to the work done a couple of decades ago by Timothy Jenkins, the practice of deliverance ministry in this diaspora community requires a certain curiosity about local categories and ways of making sense of the world, and in particular making sense of changes in the community, as when large numbers of people move from Nigeria to the area surrounding East London.

To make the central point as directly as possible: it takes less time for an evangelist to cast out demons than it takes for a GP to see a patient on a busy Thursday morning. Demons are often easier to defeat than germs.

Rowan's account may stimulate some philosophical reflections. For those who are tempted to exaggerate the significance of demons, or to suppose that there is something distinctively Christian about affirming the existence of demons (especially if a lack of such belief is taken to be a mark of 'liberal' thinking), it provides a salutary corrective: diaspora communities do not see belief in demons to be significant at all, but presuppose it. In this respect belief in demons resembles belief in emotions or electricity (or germs, to use the earlier example). All are terms for what cannot be seen but which have undoubted effects. All name phenomena that are accompanied by readily identifiable social expectations. Communities whose members have emotions expect each other to manage them, lest they be overcome by them. Those with electricity are expected to observe due caution, lest their homes become unsafe. Those with germs are expected to practise hygiene, lest they succumb to disease. To have emotions, electricity and germs is to have a threat, to have a name for it, and to have a set of practices of containment that accompany it. The same is true of demons. For communities that practice it, deliverance does not so much banish demons as contain the threat that they pose. That threat is significant, and needs action, but it is not noticeably greater than other threats: it can be dealt with in two to three minutes.

This set of brief observations may have some important implications for the Church of England (and perhaps other churches) who are grappling with how best to approach deliverance ministry. The most pressing, and perhaps most encouraging, is that for communities for whom requests for deliverance are a new or unfamiliar phenomenon there may be local communities who have many years' experience that can be drawn on. It is often wise to consult the relevant expert, and in this case such experts are likely to be members of diaspora communities.

References

Jörg Haustein, 2011, 'Embodying the spirit(s): Pentecostal demonology and deliverance discourse in Ethiopia', *Ethnos* 76.4, pp. 534–52.

Timothy Jenkins, 1999, *Religion in English Everyday Life an Ethnographic Approach*, London: Berghahn Books.

Kirsty Rowan and Karen Dwyer, 2015, 'Demonic possession and deliverance in the diaspora: phenomenological descriptions from Pentecostal deliverees', *Mental Health, Religion & Culture* 18.6, pp. 440–55.

Kirsty Rowan, 2016, '"Who are you in this body?": Identifying demons and the path to deliverance in a London Pentecostal church', *Language in Society* 45, pp. 247–70.

PART 3

Biblical Studies

7

Confronting Our Demons:
The Case of the 'Epileptic Boy'
(Mark 9.14–29)

Loveday Alexander

Both as a biblical scholar and as a preacher, I am conscious that biblical scholarship has not always done a good job at clarifying the hermeneutical processes involved in the apparently simple act of reading the Gospels in today's Church. Traditionally, biblical scholarship has focused on understanding the Gospels historically, as products of their own first-century culture. In other biblical disciplines, we are learning to confront our latent hermeneutical demons of racism, colonialism and patriarchalism – the hidden factors that still affect the way we read these ancient texts today. But when it comes to demonology, I suspect most biblical scholars would still echo the words of George Caird, writing on St Paul's 'principalities and powers' in 1957:

> As we study St Paul's teaching, we shall raise questions that carry us outside the scope of biblical scholarship. Does evil exist? Are there personal powers of evil? If so, what do we mean by 'personal'? Such questions as these I propose to leave to the philosopher. We shall also be inclined to ask how the message of the Bible on this subject is to be accommodated to modern categories of thought; but that is the function of systematic theology. Our present task is descriptive – an attempt to reconstruct something of the world of thought in which Paul's mind was at home.[1]

Since Caird's day, we have gained a much greater understanding of the historical context of the New Testament (not least through the discoveries at Qumran), as well as an increasing willingness to use the findings of anthropologists and ethnographers to illuminate magical world-views and practices today (see Davies 1995; Twelftree 1993). But the net result is to reinforce the sense of distance between the Gospel texts and the cultural and scientific assumptions of our modern world. The past – especially the biblical past – is a different country: they do things differently there. And actually it feels safer that way. We don't know what to do if denizens of that 'different country' threaten to accost us in Manchester or Birmingham today.

In this chapter, I want to illustrate the problem by looking at the episode of the 'epileptic boy' in Mark 9.14–29 and parallels (Matt. 17.14–21; Luke 9.37–42), taking the time to ask questions of the texts, and working outwards from the text to reflect on the theological issues it opens up. Matthew's version is the shortest, and in some ways the most problematic. The story tells how a man brought his epileptic son to Jesus and Jesus healed the boy by casting out a demon. At first reading, we seem to have a mismatch between diagnosis and treatment here. The child is described as an epileptic (Matt. 17.15). That sounds like a medical diagnosis, a problem you would take to a doctor. But Jesus does not act like a doctor: he treats the child's problem as a demon that needs to be expelled. Right from the start, then, we seem to have two parallel scripts for what is going on here: a medical script, inviting medical diagnosis and treatment; and a spiritual script, inviting exorcism.

But there are other troubling aspects of this case. The patient appears to have no agency. The boy (we are not told his age) is entirely passive; he is brought to Jesus by his father, and any faith (or lack of faith) in this story belongs to others – Jesus, the disciples, or (in Mark) the father. Does this give us a biblical warrant for disregarding the rights and agency of the patient? Such a reading raises the terrifying spectre of the abusive practice of subjecting epileptic patients (irrespective of their own volition) to a process of 'deliverance'. This in turn raises important issues about disability and personal identity (see Moss and Schipper 2011). It also raises problems that would today be identified as safeguarding issues.[2] And it raises a whole host of uncomfortable theological questions about the existence and ontology of spiritual beings, and about the relationship between physical and spiritual healing.

Demons and disease in the text

The first question we need to ask of this text is linguistic: what are the actual words used? 'Epilepsy' is a Greek word: but it does not appear in any of the Gospels. Matthew's word is 'moonstruck' *(seleniazetai)*, reflecting an ancient (and still widespread) medical belief linking epileptic symptoms to the phases of the moon.[3] So Matthew's story already contains an alternative, physical explanation for the boy's condition.

The next step is to look at how the story is told in the other Gospels. When we read the Gospel stories, we habitually harmonize them, but in fact they do not tell the story in the same way. Mark and Luke do not mention epilepsy. They ascribe the child's problem to a 'spirit' which 'seizes' him (neither uses the words 'demon' or 'evil'). For Luke, the spirit is 'unclean' (ritually impure). Mark describes it in terms of its effects: when it seizes the boy, he can neither speak nor hear. Either way, the story in Mark or Luke is a straightforward exorcism narrative.

Mark and Luke also give us a *medical history*, as the father describes the general pattern of the boy's condition, and the *presenting symptoms*, as the boy suffers a seizure in Jesus' presence. Jesus' procedure for eliciting the child's symptoms recalls the practice of ancient doctors, who made careful use of systematic questioning to build up a medical history (from the Greek *historia*, enquiry) (Temkin 1994, p. 49). Together, this gives us an unusually full cluster of symptoms: falling, seizure, violent convulsions, loud cries, foaming at the mouth, grinding teeth, rigidity, temporary loss of speech and hearing. This sounds very like the symptoms associated with epilepsy (pp. 36–47). We cannot get rid of the 'epileptic' label so easily.

But in many cultures around the world today, a similar set of phenomena would invite a diagnosis of spirit-possession. For a modern ethnographer or anthropologist, 'agitated forms of behaviour … can be categorized as indexes of possession, such as vomiting, crying, falling to the floor, shaking, and convulsing' (Rowan 2016, pp. 250–51). Anthropologists observe that such states are often associated with marginal groups experiencing oppression or restriction in their daily lives: 'Spirit-possession is often a way that certain individuals work around restrictions imposed by their economic, sexual, or social status, and so it will most often be found in societies where those restrictions are rather clearly defined' (Davies 1995, p. 40) – or among sub-groups (such as women) whose lives are subject to particular restrictions. At the phenomenological level, then, the Gospel story gives us an ambivalent set of symptoms that can bear a number of different diagnoses.

Demons and disease in ancient Mediterranean culture

The next question is: how did ancient Mediterranean culture read symptoms like this? The ancients did not attribute all diseases to the work of demons. Even within the New Testament, diseases and demons can be distinguished.[4] In this particular case, the differential diagnosis runs right through the ancient evidence.

1   The Hippocratic treatise *On the Sacred Disease* (c.400 BCE) describes a set of symptoms remarkably similar to Mark's: 'convulsions, severe shaking, loss of normal consciousness and control over one's body, and foaming at the mouth' (Martin 2004, p. 37). These symptoms were associated with a condition known in antiquity as 'the sacred disease'. The accepted view was that the 'sacred disease' was caused

by 'a god or *daimon* "polluting" the body of the victim'. Sometimes the disease itself was simply described as 'the *daimon*' (p. 38). Popular remedies included a mixture of 'purifications and charms': spells, sacrifice, ritual baths, and the ritual disposal of pollutants (pp. 38–9; see also Temkin 1994, pp. 7–23). Jesus' treatment would have made perfect sense to most readers within this cultural world.

2 But the author of the Hippocratic treatise argues that this condition is no more 'divine' or 'sacred' than any other disease. It is a hereditary physical condition originating in the membranes of the brain: 'the god is not the cause, nor are the purifications the remedy' (§2). This is a minority view, even among intellectuals. But it is clear that even in the ancient world there was (at least for those who could afford it) a more rationalistic, 'scientific' pathway of diagnosis and treatment for this condition.[5]

As Dale Martin points out, this is not a simple dichotomy between 'rational' medicine and religion (2004, p. 42). The author of *On the Sacred Disease* is highly religious. He argues that *all* diseases result from environmental forces (cold, sun, winds) which are themselves divine: so this disease is no more (and no less) divine than any other: 'All are divine, and all are human'. He is not against traditional religious practices like prayer and sacrifice. What he rejects is an 'impious' view that sees the disease as a personal attack by a particular deity and seeks to combat it by coercive control (pp. 43–5). The fissures in this text open along the fault-line of 'religion vs superstition/magic' rather than along the post-enlightenment fault-line of 'religion vs science'. *On the Sacred Disease* offers a valuable window into two different ways of interpreting the same symptoms in the ancient world, by the intellectual elite and in popular culture. This popular sub-culture was often dismissed by the elite as 'superstition', and is not well represented in literary texts: but our knowledge of it has grown exponentially from the study of non-literary evidence on magic and demonology across the Hellenistic and

Jewish worlds, including the Greek magical papyri, the Dead Sea Scrolls, amulets and incantation bowls.[6]

What is striking is how well the Gospels fit into this popular world-view. Within this framework, it makes perfect sense that most of the characters in the story (including Jesus) interpret the boy's symptoms as the result of demonic activity (New Testament *daimonion* is a diminutive of the Greek *daimon*, a divine being). Matthew's 'moonstruck' sounds a bit closer to the rationalism of *On the Sacred Disease*, but since the moon is equally a divine force, the effect is the same. The influence (wherever it comes from) is clearly unwelcome, scary and destructive. Jesus never challenges this view of the problem: he simply deals with it within the diagnostic framework of the culture, as an unclean spirit that needs to be expelled.

Demons and disease in the Gospel narrative

How does this story fit within the larger narrative world of the Gospels? All the Gospels (including John) interpret Jesus' story as a prolonged spiritual conflict, culminating in the apparent defeat of Judas' betrayal and Jesus' death on the cross. Jesus' death and resurrection is the ultimate victory over the forces of evil (cf. Col. 2.15). So from the outset, Jesus' power over demons and disease is a clear indication of the coming of God's Kingdom and the ultimate defeat of Satan (Mark 3.20–30 and parallels). Jesus' power over demons and disease is integrally linked to the narrative of salvation (Acts 10.38).

But the Gospel writers are also keen to defend Jesus against the accusation of magic (which was a standard feature of Jewish-Christian debate). So it is important in the story that Jesus expels the demon by a simple word of command, without the need for magical incantations.[7] Jesus' practice is both like and unlike the practice of his contemporaries. He does not challenge the basic presuppositions at work in his culture: he deals with the problem as it is perceived by those affected. Yet

Jesus also offers an implied critique of the socio-religious structures that caused the problem in the first place; and there are hints that he models a restorative therapeutic programme that offers a way out of the recurrent cycle of affliction (Davies 1995, pp. 107–12; Klutz 2004, pp. 131–32, 137–43).

But why does this particular exorcism appear precisely here in the Gospel story? Matthew, Mark and Luke all place it right at the centre of the narrative, directly after Peter's confession 'You are the Christ' (Mark 8.27–30 and parallels). Thus it is sandwiched between the revelation of Jesus' divine glory in the transfiguration (Mark 9.2–8 and parallels), and the passion predictions pointing forward to the cross (Mark 8.31–8, 9.30–2 and parallels). In Mark, the heightened atmosphere of conflict surrounding the story foreshadows the looming spiritual conflict of the passion, where Jesus himself (like the boy at the centre of the story) will become a corpse and will ultimately be resurrected.[8] All three versions highlight the peculiar difficulty of this exorcism and Jesus' own vulnerability ('How much longer must I put up with you?'; Mark 9.19; Matt. 17.17; Luke 9.41). Perhaps we can see here another foreshadowing of the passion – an involuntary groaning recognition of the personal cost of the road to the cross. Dealing with the evils that afflict humanity at every level, physical and spiritual, will require more than a display of exorcistic fireworks.[9]

Demons and disease in the Hebrew Bible

How does the demonology of the Gospels fit into the broader biblical worldview? The radical monotheism of the Hebrew Bible is highly resistant to dualism and prefers to attribute the origins of evil to God: 'Shall there be evil in the city, and I the Lord have not done it?'[10] Thus, for example, sickness in the Psalms is normally attributed to God (sometimes but not always as a result of sin), though the popular belief in sickness as a demonic force surfaces occasionally (as in Ps. 91.5–6). Trafficking with magic and the spirits of the dead is forbidden (Deut.

18:9–14). Yet the Hebrew Bible shows a remarkable lack of interest in developing a coherent demonology. Genesis offers an explanation for the origins of evil on the human level (pain, toil, shame), but there is no coherent account of the cosmic origins of evil – a gap supplied by intertestamental texts such as the books of Enoch (Alexander 1999).

The radical monotheism of the biblical texts also has implications for the theological understanding of other gods. The dominant biblical critique of the pagan gods is that they are 'idols', i.e. inert and ineffective blocks of wood (Ps. 115.4–8, 135.15–18). But in the late Hellenistic period (around 200 BCE) the Greek Bible (LXX) begins to describe the pagan gods as *daimonia* (demons), implying that they have some kind of spiritual power, though it is subordinate to the power of God.[11] But these subordinate powers are not necessarily evil. In the book of Daniel, they are angelic powers, subject to the one God but entrusted with divine authority over the nations. Worshipping these subordinate deities is forbidden to the people of Israel, because they have direct access to the sovereign God; but is not necessarily wrong for the pagan nations themselves (Caird 1957, pp. 5–15).

Demons and disease in the New Testament

The Gospel narratives are much closer than the Hebrew Bible to the popular world of Greek demonology. In a world full of conflicts and constraints, 'demons' or 'unclean spirits' provide an explanatory framework ready to hand for the multiple ills that can afflict ordinary people – perhaps reflecting an experience of 'internal exile' and marginalization, especially for women (Davies 1995, pp. 36–40; Klutz 2004, p. 132). But despite the parallels, the New Testament shows key differences from some of the widespread assumptions of demonology across the Greco-Roman world. It is solidly rooted in the theological framework emerging in late Second Temple Judaism.

The main difference is that the *daimonia* in the New Testament are not a confused crowd of hostile deities to be placated piecemeal by humans, but a unified 'Kingdom of Satan', opposed to the Kingdom of God. The idea that opposing the Kingdom of God is a kingdom of evil, ruled over by Satan, assisted by demons and fallen angels, first emerges clearly in late Second Temple Judaism. It underpins the worldview of the community of the Dead Sea Scrolls, which mostly refer to the angelic head of this evil empire under the name Belial. The back-story of when this kingdom was set up and how it operates is still pretty fluid (cf. Rev. 12); but the fact of its operation is presupposed all over the New Testament.

The distinction between prayer and magic continues to be important (though its boundaries may sometimes surprise us). Luke-Acts in particular draws a clear distinction between healing in the name of Jesus and the activities of the magicians. The tendency to assimilate the two was an ongoing problem, both for discipleship (cf. Acts 19) and for apologetics (cf. e.g. Origen, *Against Celsus* 1.68).

The ambiguity about idols resurfaces in Paul's rather confusing discussion of idol-meats in 1 Corinthians 8–10. Idols are 'nothing' (1 Cor. 8.4–6), but they are also *daimonia*, retaining genuine spiritual power (1 Cor. 10.19–22). Paul's 'principalities and powers' seem to be in continuity with Daniel's angelic powers, working through the structures of pagan society, a world in which the saints have no political control over their own destinies (Caird 1957, pp. 22–6). The authority of the powers is derived from God and is legitimate as long as its subordinate status is acknowledged (cf. Rom. 13).[12]

Reading the Gospels today: towards a theology of deliverance

Historical exegesis has enabled us to make huge strides in understanding the Gospels in their own cultural world. But this is merely the first step towards developing a theological framework for deliverance ministry today. Here I can only suggest a few pointers.

Jesus' practice provokes a reflection on cultural accommodation or *oikonomia.* The fact that these stories made sense within the popular worldview of their day undoubtedly contributed (historically speaking) to the popular success of the Gospel (Hull 1974, p. 142). The Incarnate Word, we might say, could only communicate within the thought-world of the day using time-bound words and concepts. This might provoke a Christological question: 'Did Jesus know the science?' is not an entirely ridiculous question. Was Jesus' accommodation to the worldview of his hearers simply part of the divine *oikonomia* of incarnation, part of the voluntary *kenosis* of the Incarnate Logos? If so, what are its implications for our pastoral practice today?

But accommodation can create problems when thought-worlds change. What makes sense within the popular worldview of the Gospels (and in many cultures worldwide) may no longer be the only option for making sense of the phenomena in today's Western world. Later generations of theologians found themselves forced to defend the 'superstition' of the Gospels against the rationalism of the intellectual elite (Temkin 1991). We live in a world that has seen significant medical advances in the analysis and treatment of epilepsy and other conditions. We cannot simply un-know what we know: if we hold theologically to the unity of truth, then the discoveries of medical science must also be factored into our theology of deliverance. One of the ways God provides deliverance is through advances in medical diagnosis and treatment – and this is just as true of epilepsy as of malaria or cancer. Vaccination programmes and the extension of medical care across poorer sections of society are also aspects of deliverance. Our theology of deliverance, like our theology of healing, must be integrated with our theology (do we have one?) of psychiatry and medicine. The Church's ministry of deliverance, like the Church's ministry of healing, must be exercised in collaboration with the work of the medical profession.[13]

Our theology of deliverance must also take account of other theological imperatives in our world: a theology of disability, a theology of the person, a theology of safeguarding. In the Church of England, any minister who is approached with a request for deliverance ministry to deal with 'behavioural problems' in a child or young person is required to contact the Diocesan Safeguarding Adviser (Church of England 2018, p. 26 (§7.6)). Social issues of power, culture and oppression may also call for theological reflection. 'Prayer for healing [and deliverance] needs to take seriously the way in which individual sickness and vulnerability are often the result of injustice and social oppression' (Church of England 2000, p. 11).

But equally, our theology of deliverance must take account of the framing narratives of biblical cosmology: radical monotheism and the resistance to dualism; a renewed and chastened understanding of the created order and the limits of human intervention; the reality of both good and evil in the spiritual world.

Above all, our theology of deliverance must be situated within a robust and holistic theology of salvation: 'Salvation, wholeness, healing and peace with God are part of the same family of words, revealing the same essential theological themes as both incarnation and crucifixion: vulnerability and powerlessness, identification and suffering, being put right, made whole and restored as part of a new creation. These gospel themes relate to the real human condition, with humility and without triumphalism, in a way that brings people face to face with Jesus Christ' (Church of England 2000, p. 4).

References

Philip S. Alexander, 1999, 'The Demonology of the Dead Sea Scrolls', in P. W. Flint and J. C. VanderKam (eds.), *The Dead Sea Scrolls After Fifty Years: A Comprehensive Assessment*, Brill: Leiden, pp. 331–53.
Sallie Baxendale and Jennifer Fisher, 2008, 'Moonstruck? The effect of the lunar cycle on seizures', *Epilepsy and Behaviour* 13.3, pp. 549–50.
Gideon Bohak, 2008, *Ancient Jewish Magic: A History*, Cambridge: Cambridge University Press.

George Caird, 1957, *Principalities and Powers*, Oxford: Clarendon Press.

The Church of England, 2000, *Pastoral Services*, London: Church House Publishing.

The Church of England, 2018, *Parish Safeguarding Handbook*, London: Church House Publishing.

Stevan Davies, 1995, *Jesus the Healer: Possession, Trance, and the Origins of Christianity*, London: SCM Press.

John Hull, 1974, *Hellenistic Magic and the Synoptic Tradition*, London: SCM Press.

Todd Klutz, 2004, *The Exorcism Stories in Luke-Acts*, SNTSMS 129; Cambridge: Cambridge University Press.

Dale Martin, 2004, *Inventing Superstition: from the Hippocratics to the Christians*, Cambridge: Harvard University Press.

Candida R. Moss and J. Schipper, 2011, *Disability Studies and Biblical Literature*, London: Palgrave Macmillan.

J. M. Ross, 1978, 'Epileptic or Moonstruck?', *The Bible Translator* 29, pp. 126–8.

Kirsty Rowan, 2016, 'Who are you in this body? Identifying demons and the path to deliverance in a London Pentecostal Church', *Language in Society* 45.2, pp. 247–70.

Owsei Temkin, 1991, *Hippocrates in a World of Pagans and Christians*, Baltimore: Johns Hopkins.

Owsei Temkin, 1994 (orig. 1945), *The Falling Sickness: A History of Epilepsy from the Greeks to the Beginnings of Modern Neurology*, Baltimore: Johns Hopkins.

Graham H. Twelftree, 1993, *Jesus the Exorcist*, WUNT 54; Tübingen, Mohr Siebeck.

Walter Wink, *Naming the Powers*, 1984; *Unmasking the Powers*, 1986; *Engaging the Powers* 1992, Philadelphia: Fortress Press.

Notes

1 Caird, pp. x–xi. Todd Klutz (2004, Introduction, p. 77cf) makes a similar point.

2 Cf. The Church of England Parish Safeguarding Handbook, p. 26 (§7.6).

3 Our word 'lunatic' (from Latin *luna*, the moon) conveys the same idea (though it has nothing to do with the patient's mental state); see Ross, pp. 126-8; Baxendale and Fisher, pp. 549-50.

4 Cf. Mark 1.32–4; Matt. 10.1,7; Luke 9.1–2 (though the boundaries within the tradition are fluid).

5 Whether it would have done the patient any good is another matter: the expertise of ancient medicine lay more in observation and diagnosis than in treatment (Temkin, pp. 23–7).

6 For a dated but still useful introduction, see Hull 1974. See further Bohak 2008, especially pp. 70–142 on 'Jewish Magic in the Second Temple Period'.

7 Klutz 2004, pp. 188–94; see also the submerged debates about the role of faith, prayer and fasting in dealing with 'this kind' (pp.199–205).

8 The boy is described in Mark first as dead (*nekros*), then as risen (*aneste*) (Mark 9.26–7). In Luke, the father describes the boy as his 'only son' (*monogenes*; Luke 9.38).

9 Cf. Matt. 12.15–20, where Jesus' healing ministry is linked with the ministry of the suffering servant.

10 Amos 3.6; cf. 1 Sam. 18.10, where Saul is afflicted by 'an evil spirit from God'.

11 Ps. 96.5 in the LXX reads 'the gods of the nations are *daimonia*'; see Caird, pp. 11–13.

12 See the works of Walter Wink for a concerted attempt to develop a theology of the powers: *Naming the Powers* (1984); *Unmasking the Powers* (1986); *Engaging the Powers* (1992).

13 Cf. *Pastoral Services*, p. 11: 'Prayer for healing and strengthening should not involve the rejection of the skills and activity of medicine which are also part of God's faithfulness to creation (Eccles. 38.9–12; Ps. 147.3).'

8

Dealing With Demons:
Jesus Among the Ancient Exorcists

Hector M. Patmore

Exorcism was one of the most prominent aspects of Jesus' public ministry. But Jesus was far from being the only itinerant Jewish exorcist at the time. How did Jesus' ministry of exorcism compare to that of his contemporaries? Which aspects of Jesus' approach to demons were distinct from that of his contemporaries? What ideas and practices did he share with his contemporaries? These are the questions we will tackle in this chapter.

Jesus' practice

Let us begin with one of the best known descriptions of an exorcism from a non-biblical source. The Jewish writer, Flavius Josephus, writing in 93 CE (around the time the Gospels of Matthew and Luke were being composed), describes an exorcism that he claims to have witnessed:

> I became acquainted with a certain Eleazar of my own people, who, in the presence of Vespasian and his sons, along with their tribunes and a crowd of soldiers, delivered those possessed by demons. The method of healing is as follows: Bringing up to the nose of the person possessed by a demon a ring that had under its seal a root from among those prescribed by Solomon, [Eleazar] would then draw out the demon through the nostrils as the man sniffed. Upon

the man's immediately falling down, he adjured the demon not to return to him again, making mention of Solomon and likewise reciting the incantations he [Solomon] had composed. (Begg and Spilsbury 2005, 1.46–8 modified)

It is often necessary to treat what Josephus says with a pinch of salt, but, although some elements of the story – the presence of emperor Vespasian, for example – might seem a little far fetched, his description of the exorcism itself seems quite plausible in light of other ancient Jewish sources.

When we look at the building-blocks of the narrative, we see that structurally there are some similarities between Josephus's account and those found in the Gospels. Much as the Gospels do, Josephus begins setting the scene by introducing the characters in the story:

- The exorcist, Eleazar, who in this case is a Jew (that is what Josephus means by 'of my own people'). In the Gospel accounts, Jesus fulfils this role.
- The victim: an anonymous figure who has been possessed by a demon.
- The witnesses: Vespasian, his sons, the soldiers, and perhaps Josephus himself. The Gospel accounts normally mention a crowd, or family members of the possessed individual, or Jesus' opponents, who function as the witnesses (e.g. Matt. 8.28–34; Mark 5.1–13; Luke 8.26–36; Matt. 12.22–32; Mark 3.19–30; Luke 11.14–26; Mark 7.24–30; cf. Matt. 15.21–8; Matt. 17.14–20; Mark 9.17–29; Luke 9.37–42; Mark 1.21–7; Luke 4.31–6; Mark 9.17, 20, 25).

Comparing the Gospel accounts to this account from Josephus also highlights a number of features that are quite different:

- First, in Josephus's story there are magical *objects* and *substances*: there is ring that contains the root of a certain plant; elsewhere Josephus describes where such roots come from, how dangerous they are, and how to harvest them without coming to harm (i.e. War 7.185).

- Then there are fixed forms of words – *'incantations'* composed by Solomon – that have an effect on the demon.

- Josephus also says that Eleazar made 'mention of Solomon', by which he means that the exorcist invoked the *name* of an individual regarded as having power over demons; the very act of invoking this power-figure helps drive the demon away.

- And, finally, Eleazar performs various *actions*: he waves the ring under the victim's nose, then pulls to get the demon out.

Some of these elements also appear in accounts of exorcism in the New Testament. The Book of Acts, for example, tells us about the use of *magical objects*: it reports that during his third missionary journey, 'God did extraordinary miracles by the hands of Paul, so that handkerchiefs or aprons were carried away from his [Paul's] body to the sick, and diseases left them and *the evil spirits came out of them*' (Acts 19.12).

Likewise, Jesus' name was used by his followers to cast out demons (see Mark 16.17–18; Luke 10.17–20) in the same way that Eleazar uses Solomon's name in Josephus's account. The Book of Acts tells of the sons of Sceva who try (unsuccessfully) to cast out demons by saying 'I adjure you *by the Jesus* whom Paul preaches' (Acts 19.13, cf. Acts 19.15–16); Paul himself casts the spirit out of a slave girl with the words: 'I charge you *in the name of Jesus Christ* to come out of her'; the Book of Acts reports that the spirit 'came out that very moment' (Acts 16.18).

Although the contemporaries of Jesus and his followers make use of these practices, Jesus himself does not do any of these things when he performs exorcisms: he does not make use of objects, substances, or particular actions; he does not recite incantations; and he does not invoke powerful names (Twelftree 1993, pp. 157–65). Instead, Jesus simply speaks with the demons and instructs them (or permits them) to leave. In contrast, Jesus does use substances and particular actions in healings that have no explicit demonic cause (e.g. spittle, laying on hands; Mark 7.33, 8.23; John 9.6), pointing to the belief that, though demons were thought to be able to cause physical impairments (hence the 'dumb and deaf spirit' in Mark 9.25), not all such maladies were thought to be caused by demons.

Jesus does things differently. The Gospels stress that the Jesus is not the same as all the other practitioners of exorcism because he has a different kind of mission and authority. Right after his very first exorcism in Mark's Gospel, for example, the crowd react in amazement, saying, 'What is this? A new teaching! *With authority* he commands even the unclean spirits, and they obey him' (Mark 1.27). Jesus does not need to call on the authority of Solomon, for example, because his own authority was greater that Solomon's (cf. Matt. 12.42; Luke 11.31). The Gospels, of course, link this special authority with the coming of the Kingdom, in other words with the arrival of a new age in human history – a climactic stage in history – in which God was acting in a decisive way through Jesus to bring about the end of evil (Mark 3.27; Matt. 12.28–29; Luke 11.20–21).

The underlying ideas

Let us explore this last theme in a little more depth, because these underlying ideas need to remain central as we reflect on how we approach deliverance as a distinctly Christian form of ministry. I want to use one of the most famous exorcism stories in the Gospel to take us a bit deeper into this topic:

> They came to the other side of the sea, to the country of the Gerasenes. And when [Jesus] had come out of the boat, there met him out of the tombs a man with an unclean spirit ... And when he saw Jesus from afar, he ran and worshiped him; and crying out with a loud voice, he said, "What have you to do with me, Jesus, Son of the Most High God? I adjure you by God, do not torment me."

For he had said to him, "Come out of the man, you unclean spirit!"
And Jesus asked him, "What is your name?" He replied, "My name
is Legion; for we are many." And he begged him eagerly not to send
them out of the country. Now a great herd of swine was feeding
there on the hillside; and they begged him, "Send us to the swine,
let us enter them." So he gave them leave. And the unclean spirits
came out, and entered the swine; and the herd, numbering about
two thousand, rushed down the steep bank into the sea, and were
drowned in the sea. (Mark 5.1–13, RSV)

As scholars have long recognized, there are a number of features in this
text that allude to the Romans. Most obviously, the demons identify
themselves as 'Legion', which is the name of a unit of troops in the
Roman army; one of the legions active in the region at that time was
Legio X Fretensis, which happened to use the image of a boar on its
heraldry (where do the demons go once they leave the man?!). What are
we to make of this?

One popular line of argument has been to suggest that in one way
or another the demons symbolize the Roman authorities, so that the
story is really a metaphor intended to serve as anti-Roman propaganda
(e.g. Marcus 2000, pp. 341–53; Myers 1988, pp. 190–4). I do not think
this does justice to the ancient content of the narrative. This line of
interpretation presupposes that the story is *either* about demons *or* it
is about Romans. But I do not think the first readers of Mark's Gospel
would have thought in terms of 'either/or'. To the audience for whom
Mark wrote, Romans and the demons were simply two sides of the same
coin. For them, the story would not be about Romans *or* demons, but
about Romans *and* demons. What do I mean by that?

A number of ancient Jewish sources reflect in various ways the idea
that the organization of the human realm – the visible realm – reflects
the structure of the supernatural realm. One can trace this idea back to
the book of Deuteronomy (32.8–9), in which it is said that God 'fixed

the bounds of the peoples according to the number of the sons of God (= angels)' (Dan. 12.1; Isa. 24.21–3). The idea that each nation or ethnic group was under the rule of a guardian angel ultimately developed into the belief that the righteous were under the rule of God and his angels, whereas everyone else was under the rule of an arch-demon (familiar to us under the name 'Satan'), and the demons, who served as his foot-soldiers and henchmen (see for example the Book of Jubilees 15.30–2). In this understanding of the cosmos, all the evil-doers – whether supernatural or natural, visible or not – form a single front, an alliance. The Kingdom of God was ranged against this 'Kingdom' of Satan.

Jesus' *practices* may have differed from those of his Jewish contemporaries, as we have seen, but this notion of a cosmos in conflict is rather similar to concepts found in other Jewish sources. I want to illustrate this point with an example from the Dead Sea Scrolls. The Dead Sea Scrolls are a group of manuscripts that were found in caves in the Judean desert, most of which date from between the second century BCE and the first century CE. Among these manuscripts was a text called the War Scroll, which contains a prophecy about a climactic war that will bring an end to evil. What is of interest for us is that the War Scroll envisages humans and supernatural beings all fighting together: 'On that day the company of divine beings and the assembly of human-beings shall engage one another (in battle),' it says, 'resulting in great carnage' (1QM 1.10). So, according to the War Scroll, on one side of the battle there are the righteous, who the text calls the 'Sons of Light'; with the help of God the Sons of Light fight against 'the army' of the chief demon, called Belial in the text (cf. 2 Cor. 6.15), his angels, and humans under his control, including worldly powers such as the Romans.

The important point is this: had this battle ever taken place, the combatants might have found themselves fighting Roman soldiers but they would have understood themselves to be participating in a fight against demonic forces: they fought alongside angels and against demons. Somewhat similar ideas are also found in the Book of Revelation, in which 'demonic spirits' are described as bringing together 'the kings of the whole world ... for battle on the great day of God the Almighty' (Rev. 16.14; cf. Jude 1.9). Demons were the driving force behind the Romans.

Returning to Jesus' exorcism of the Legion of demons, we can now see the story in a new light. If the story is merely a *metaphor* about overcoming political oppression, then I doubt it would have been terribly encouraging. I think Mark's first readers would probably have responded with a shrug of the shoulders and an apathetic *'plus ça change!'* The situation of Jews under Roman rule was much worse when Mark wrote his Gospel than it was in Jesus' day; it would have been hard to see that much had been achieved in terms of alleviating Roman oppression. But if we take demons and Romans to be two sides of the same coin, things look rather different. In the eyes of many ancient Jews, the Romans were merely the symptoms of which demons were the underlying cause.

Implications for the ministry of deliverance

Let me try and sum up in a few words and offer some reflections on what this might imply for the Christian ministry of deliverance.

Jesus carried out his exorcisms in a way that was distinct from the practices of his contemporaries because he embodied a kind of authority that other exorcists simply did not have and was engaged in a much more fundamental project, namely, preparing the way for the Kingdom of God. The story of the Gerasenes demoniac sheds light on the assumptions about the demonic realm that lay behind this practice, and which Jesus shared with some of his contemporaries. Like his contemporaries, Jesus probably took the view that some (but not all) of the troubles and afflictions experienced in the human realm were ultimately caused by forces that are 1) beyond human control, and 2) not an expression of the will of God. These forces are called demons. The activity of demons therefore reflects a fundamental disordering of the entire cosmos (i.e. the created order). The cosmos is not as it should be; Jesus begins the process of re-ordering the cosmos in his ministry; once that work is completed, creation will have been renewed and will be a full expression of the will of God. This is the Kingdom of God.

What might some of the implications of this be for the Christian ministry of deliverance?

First and foremost, these observations suggest that deliverance belongs not to the margins of Christian theology but to its centre – exactly where it stood in Jesus' ministry and the early Church (Twelftree 2007), and where it still stands in the majority of churches globally. Put simply, deliverance is part of the work of preparing the way for the Kingdom to come it its fullness. As such, the texts we have reflected on caution us against always treating demons as a *localized* problem.

Let me elaborate on this point by returning to the story in Mark. A common post-colonial interpretation of this passage understands the Gerasenes demoniac's mental disturbance to be a consequence of the brutal Roman military occupation (see e.g. Sugirtharajah 2009, pp. 91–4; Hogeterp 2020). According to this theory, the victim has internalized traumatic experiences, or perhaps his hostility towards the occupier, resulting in a dissociative disorder. For the ancient Jewish reader, this would not be removed from the realm of demonic activity, since the Romans were understood to owe their power to the demons. Since demons may be at work at the individual, local, or systemic levels, the demons would simply be regarded as working *through* the Romans to provoke the victim's mental disturbance. Transfer this to our times and there remains no shortage of environmental stressors that have a detrimental effect on mental health: deprivation, inequality, exploitation – tragically, the list goes on. For some whose experience reflects that of the Gerasenes demoniac, a rite of exorcism modelled on the practice of Jesus in this particular story might prove beneficial. But for many, deliverance will mean tackling the structural causes of their distress through which the demons are at work. In these cases, deliverance could well mean driving out the demons not from individuals *per se* but from the unjust social systems that torment them.

This leads on to another important point, namely that we cannot treat deliverance in isolation from the broader mandate to heal (e.g. Matt. 10.8; Luke 10.8–9). For some, a rite of exorcism may be appropriate or helpful, but for others, it might prove ineffective or even harmful. As Toensing has pointed out, if we treat this story as *paradigmatic* for understanding the causes (possession) and appropriate response (exorcism) to individuals that manifest the same symptoms as the Gerasenes demoniac, such as self-harm (see Mark 5.5), then this story risks becoming 'spiritually alienating' for those affected by mental illness for whom 'exorcism' does not provide a cure. The same would be true of many other similar stories in the Gospel. The tale of the Gerasenes demoniac is a narrative about a particular individual, not a prescription for universal application. Furthermore, we should we not lose sight of the fact that the exorcist in this story has a power and authority like no other, for it is none other than God incarnate who brings the Gerasenes demoniac to his right mind. What is possible for God is not always possible for human beings (Matt. 19.26; Mark 10.27; Luke 18.27); we may therefore have to work differently to ensure that the ministry we carry out is healing rather than harming.

Adopting the cultural categories of Mark's narrative itself, I have spoken throughout of 'demons', 'demonic' and the 'demoniac'. Since many find this language to be extremely problematic, a word or two on this topic is perhaps in order. It is all too easy to get hung up on questions like 'do demons really exist?' or 'are demons really *beings* as such?' – what we might call the 'ontological stumbling-block' if you will excuse some jargon. But we cannot simply 'demythologize' the biblical language or treat it as merely metaphorical without finding ourselves guilty of a kind of ideological colonialism (Wiebe 2011). For some, this terminology is a meaningful category within a particular culture; for others, such nomenclature more accurately captures their own personal experience of self-alienation than any other choice of words. These positions cannot be dismissed, denigrated, or silenced. I find it helpful to reflect on the biblical texts in wrestling with this issue, because the Bible itself is not terribly interested in questions about the essence of demons. Rather, it uses the language of 'demons' to speak of forces that are beyond human control, work against the will of God, and have tangible consequences in our world. Whether or not these are 'beings' as such seems to be a moot point. The more pressing questions for the biblical authors were how one counteracts such forces and how they fit in to God's larger plan for the cosmos. The ontology of demons is therefore a matter that can perhaps best be held in suspense, in order to maintain a focus on these more urgent matters.

Drawing these threads together, these reflections point to the need for sensitivity and discernment in the Christian ministry of deliverance: how and where are demons at work and how can they best be dealt with? How does our ministry contribute to the process of putting the order of the cosmos right again? Is the ministry we offer appropriate and helpful to the individual involved? For those called to exercise this ministry, wrestling with these questions might require them to enter territory – either literal or metaphorical – that feels alien. Jesus, of course, does just this in the case of Gerasenes demoniac, crossing over to an unfamiliar region, to seek out an individual who is isolated and in agony, and to bring to him the power of the Kingdom. Deliverance is a tangible sign of the Kingdom putting forth its leaves; it points us forward to the perfection of the Kingdom, when this work will be completed. In this our hope lies.

References

Christopher T. Begg and Paul Spilsbury (trans.), 2005, Josephus Flavius, *Judean antiquities* 8–10, Leiden: Brill.

Albert Hogeterp, 2020, 'Trauma and its Ancient Literary Representation: Mark 5,1–20', *Zeitschrift für die Neutestamentliche Wissenschaft* 111.1, pp. 1–32.

Joel Marcus, 2000, *Mark 1–8: A New Translation with Introduction and Commentary*, New York: Doubleday.

Ched Myers, 1988, *Binding the Strong Man: A Political Reading of Mark's Story of Jesus*, Maryknoll, NY: Orbis.

Rasiah S. Sugirtharajah, 2009, *Postcolonial Criticism and Biblical Interpretation*, Oxford: Oxford University Press.

Holly Joan Toensing, 2007, '"Living among the Tombs": Society, Mental Illness, and Self-Destruction in Mark 5:1-20', in Hector Avalos (ed.), *This Abled Body: Rethinking Disabilities in Biblical Studies*, Atlanta, GA: Society of Biblical Literature, pp.131–43.

Graham H. Twelftree, 1993, *Jesus the Exorcist*, Tübingen: Mohr Siebeck.

Graham H. Twelftree, 2007, *In the Name of Jesus: Exorcism among Early Christians*, Grand Rapids, MI: Baker Academic.

Gregory David Wiebe, 2011, 'The Demonic Phenomena of Mark's "Legion": Evaluating Postcolonial Understandings of Demon Possession', in Anna Runesson (ed.), *Exegesis in the Making: Postcolonialism and New Testament Studies*, Leiden: Brill, pp. 186–212.

Further reading

Richard A. Horsley, 2001, *Hearing the Whole Story: The Politics of Plot in Mark's Gospel*, Louisville, KY: Westminster John Knox.

Hans Leander, 2013, *Discourses of Empire: The Gospel of Mark from a Postcolonial Perspective*, Atlanta, GA: Society of Biblical Literature.

9

Exploitation, Exorcism and Power: Reconfiguring Culpability for Possession in the New Testament

Candida R. Moss

This essay concerns and explores biblical stories that discuss the exploitation and mistreatment of those identified as possessed in the Gospel of Luke and Acts. It holds in tension two sets of concerns, both of which centre on our ethical commitments to others. The first is a commitment to the rights of disabled people, whose conditions have historically been misunderstood as signs of sin, spiritual failure, or demonic possession and who have, as a result, been mistreated, maligned and ostracized. The second is a concern for the ways in which various forms of religiosity and certain liminal figures are stereotyped as superstitious, dangerous and magical. These caricatures – which are deeply racialized and gendered – can equally affect those who cultivate spiritual gifts, those who practice exorcism, *and* those who receive exorcisms and spiritual deliverance. From among these two groups women, ethnic and racial minorities, people with disabilities and outsiders are especially susceptible to the accusation that they are superstitious, engaged in 'primitive religious practices', or spiritually possessed.

In 2013 I attended the Vatican's semi-famous course on Exorcism and Deliverance ministry at the Pontifical Athenaeum Regina Apostolorum in Rome. One thing I took away from the experience was the realization that no official exorcism takes place without psychiatric approval and medical involvement. No one ends up in the exorcist's chair without first spending time on the psychiatrist's couch. At the same time, I worried about some of the subjects in the case studies and I was troubled by the way that the conversation about possession focused almost exclusively on the culpability of the victim. To my mind, the early Christian evidence presents a more complicated picture, one in which others benefit from, exploit, and produce demonic possession. Thus, in this essay I will focus on this larger swathe of actors and institutional structures. My hope is that broadening the conversation will create possibilities for practical steps that respect both the rights of disabled people and the integrity of deliverance ministries. In doing so I will focus primarily on two stories from the Lukan corpus: the story of the enslaved girl with the Pythian spirit in Acts 16 and the story of the Gerasene demoniac from Luke 8.

Ancient anthropology

Before turning to Luke, however, it is useful for me to offer a brief note on medical anthropology in antiquity. While this essay is not interested in *how* it is that people become possessed, it is worth noting that ancient thought maintained that anyone was liable to spiritual possession. Ancient popular medicine saw sickness as something that invaded the body. In this model, disease is seen as an alien entity, it is caused by external factors that attack and pollute the body. According to classical medical writers like Celsus, invasion etiology was common 'in the old days' and among 'the people', who believed that disease was the result of an attack by the gods or *daimonian* (*On medicine* 4). This invasion etiology focused on the strength of the boundaries of the body. In modern parlance we might refer to this as the immune system. In ancient thought the focus was on the surface of the body, which like a permeable membrane, could allow things to move in and out of it. As orifices, these pores (*poroi*) allowed external matter to enter our bodies for destructive purposes. The more porous a person was the more vulnerable they were to invasion. For a variety of reasons related to masculinity, anyone who was 'unmanly' – that is to say women, sick people, enslaved persons, passive actors in sexual encounters, and so on – were supposed to be especially porous.

Even though porosity and vulnerability to invasion were the cause of disease, unboundedness was not always a bad thing. In disability studies we would call this the distinction between impairment and disability. An impairment, in this case porosity, becomes disabling only when one becomes physically or spiritually sick. There are other contexts in which being porous might be spiritually advantageous. The descent of the Holy Spirit at Pentecost endows the Apostles with some enviable language skills (Acts 2.4). And, as I have argued elsewhere, the woman with the flow of blood who reaches out and clasps the hem of Jesus' garment in Mark is healed precisely because both she and Jesus have porous bodies (Mark 5.25–34; Moss 2010).

Porosity and bodily openness to supernatural contact underpins a great deal of ancient baptismal ritual thought. For early Christians, baptism and the receipt of the Holy Spirit at baptism through the laying on of hands, utilizes the same biological pathways as demonic possession. For this reason, in the early Church, as today in many denominations, baptism was prefigured by what is sometimes called a 'minor' or 'simple exorcism'. Ancient liturgies like the second century CE *Apostolic Tradition* attributed to Hippolytus of Rome presuppose that all human beings are susceptible to spiritual possession. The important thing, then, is that the only entity that is resident inside you is the Holy Spirit, who does not tolerate malevolent housemates. This is exactly why early liturgical texts prohibit catechumens from exchanging the kiss of the peace: 'their kiss is not yet pure'. If they are possessed by an unholy spirit, they could contaminate everyone else (*Apostolic Tradition* 18.3).

This whirlwind summary has two purposes: to normalize human vulnerability to spiritual possession and to note that the same human frailties that make us vulnerable to attack also empower us to commune with one another and with the divine. With all of this in mind let us turn to two well-known stories of demonic possession from the writings of Luke.

The girl with the Pythian spirit (Acts 16.16–24)

During a whirlwind tour of Asia Minor and Macedonia, Paul and Silas found themselves in the Roman colony of Philippi staying at the residence of Lydia, a newly baptized merchant who delt in highly coveted textiles coloured with exclusive purple dye. After weeks of arduous travel, the two travellers decided to remain at Lydia's home for some time. One day they encountered an unusual girl on the street; she was an enslaved prophet who was possessed by a 'Pythian spirit' (16.16 in Greek a *pneuma Pythona*). The girl's supernatural abilities were monetized by her enslavers, who had put her to work as a street fortune-teller. Prophecy, however, is not so neatly circumscribed: when she saw Paul and his companions, she began to follow them announcing to anyone that would listen that they were 'slaves of the Most High God, who proclaim to you a way of salvation' (Acts 16.17). Each day when the small group of Jesus followers passed by her the same thing would happen. Paul, however, was not pleased by the unsolicited publicity for his evangelical work. Worn-down and irritated by this unwanted religious competitor, Paul snapped and exorcised the demon from the girl.

The girl, or rather the powerful spirit controlling her, had not asked for an exorcism but, more importantly for Paul, neither had its allies – her enslavers and oracular pimps. Enraged by the sudden loss of revenue they hauled the Apostle to court and brought a successful lawsuit against him. The girl is voiceless as she is tossed between the competing wills of the spirit that possesses her, the enslavers who exploit her, and the Apostle who exorcises her. What her story directs us to is a particular kind of ancient religiosity that, as Dan-el Padilla Peralata has written, was feared, valued and associated with enslaved people: frenzied divination. And what everyone, from Roman emperors to early Christian authors, agreed upon was that whatever the source of the divination, it worked.

In one of his moments of taxonomic classism, the elite Roman senator Cicero wrote that there were two kinds of divination in the world: what he calls artificial divination and natural divination. Artificial divination was learned, it was practiced by religious experts who may well have crafted charismatic personae for themselves but nevertheless grounded their skills in deduction and conjecture. Natural divination, in his opinion, was a different species entirely. Though, like other forms of divination, it predicted the future, it was rooted in the body and the body's potential connection to supernatural beings (*On divination* 1.25–26). It was because the bodies of liminal people – women and enslaved people – lacked the rigid impermeability of self-controlled freeborn men that they were susceptible to possession and more open to communication with the divine. As Dan-el Padilla Peralta (2017) has written, the frenzy of the socially marginalized was threatening to those in power. Though they utilized enslaved diviners to predict the future, elites were made anxious by the unregulated potency and charisma of such individuals. Columella recommended that his fellow estate-owners keep enslaved prophets off their farms (*On rural affairs* 1.8.6). The legal contracts that governed the sale of enslaved people specified that vendors disclose those disorders that might read as possession, but Roman law did not allow enslavers to complain if their workers turned out to 'associate with religious fanatics and joins in their utterances' (*Digest* 21.1.9–10).

We do not know the girl's name, much less her story, perhaps she had been trafficked to Philippi to cater to the oracular needs of the wealthy Italian ex-pat and veteran community that lived there. Was she, like the Gerasene demoniac, chained up and isolated when she was not prophesying? Or was she always working? The topography of Roman plays suggests that the area worked by dream interpreters, lot diviners and fortune tellers abutted the ancient red-light-district. Young, enslaved women were always vulnerable, and special skills did not offer protection. Even psychic royalty like the Trojan princess Cassandra could wind up as enslaved sex workers.

The name 'Pythian spirit' calls to mind the oracle at Delphi associated in myth with Apollo. The 'Pythia' were young girls who served as Apollo's spokeswomen. Though they were, by convention, virgins, the mechanics of the oracle were suggestive: the oracle was a fissure in the ground through which divinatory steam was emitted. The Pythia would sit on a tripod atop the steam vent and as the steam rose up under her skirt would deliver the message of the god to an interpreter. It was, we might say, divination through supernatural sexual assault. The mechanics of the oracle meant that it could only work at Delphi, perhaps the invocation of the name in Acts suggests that she is vulnerable to all kinds of unwanted bodily possession. If she was, like the Pythia of Delphi, a virgin then Paul's exorcism had removed whatever protections she had formerly enjoyed. Once Paul had expelled the celebrity spirit and eliminated one income stream, her enslavers would almost certainly have sex trafficked her instead. In the battle between Paul and the spirit of Apollo, the young woman in some important ways is the loser.

Gerasene demoniac (Luke 8.26–39)

With that let us turn to an earlier story from the Lukan oeuvre, the man from Gerasa typically known as the Gerasene demoniac, Legion, or the Man with the Legion in Luke 8. This story differs in some important ways from the version in Mark. When we encounter the man, he is disenfranchised and alone. Naked and homeless he is living on the margins of society in the tombs. He is experiencing what historian of slavery Orlando Patterson (2018) has called 'social death': he has been expelled from the community and realm of humanity. Though alive he is also socially dead and has been forced into an extreme condition of solitary confinement. That the man longs for human contact is clear from the fact that he goes out to meet Jesus in Luke 8.27. Jesus commands the unclean spirit to leave the man, asks him his name, and expels the legion of spirits into a nearby herd of pigs who, as we all know, rush to their deaths off a nearby cliff. There is much to unpack in the story about the mechanics of exorcism and the importance of naming demons, but I want to avoid the flashier elements of the story and focus on the actions of the absent inhabitants of Gerasa.

When Jesus encounters the man his first words are 'do not torture me' (8.28). Traditional lines of interpretation read this passage as a statement by the demonic Legion, but subjectivity is difficult to parse in this passage. It's hard to pin down who acts where: the passive verbs suggest that the demon seizes him and drives him out into the wild, but he is said to speak and break shackles. Grammatical ambiguities muddy and muddle our sense of subjectivity and that is probably the point. What is underexplored here is the backstory. According to 8.29, a Lukan supplement to Mark's version, when the man was seized by the demon, others – presumably his neighbours, friends and family members – would bind him with chains and shackles and keep him under guard. We do not know who they are because the actions also take place in the passive mood. Much like the legion of demons they act upon the man and do things to him.

Traditionally, we explain the reference to shackling and binding as a form of self-defence. The Gerasene, it is assumed, was in some way a danger to others or himself and, thus, was confined and isolated for 'his own good' or for the good of other members of his community. I should note that this is not explicit in the story. We do not know what is implied by the phrase the 'demon seized him' (8.29) and we do not know anything that happened to him before his neighbours performed their brutal intervention. But what we do know is what happens to people who are shackled, cut off from society, and forced into solitary confinement. As Luis Ménendez-Antuña has written in a beautiful article on solitary confinement and the Gerasene demoniac, these experiences are a form of torture. Those placed in conditions like those of the demoniac, he writes, often experience extreme psychological side effects that 'distort, undo, unhinge and unglue subjectivity' (2019, p. 651).

Victims of this kind of social death feel detachment from their own bodies and identities and even an inability to recall their own names. In his autobiography, *In the Belly of the Beast*, American Jack Abbott describes his experience of being confined to a blackout cell (a small room with no light): 'I heard someone screaming far way and it was me. I fell against the wall, and as if it were a catapult, was hurled across the cell to the opposite wall. Back and forth I reeled, from the door to the walls, screaming. Insane' (Abbott 1982, p. 27).

Other former prisoners describe the experience of radical separation from sociality as 'choking' them and trying to 'squeeze sanity' from their mind. The effects of solitary confinement as documented in numerous scientific studies include hallucinations, paranoia, post-traumatic stress disorder, uncontrollable rage, self-harm and mutilation, diminished impulse control, and distortions of time and perception. These effects are particularly damaging for those with pre-existing mental illness, particularly those who are young. The research of University of Nottingham criminologist Philippa Tomczak confirms that in the UK population people with mental illness who are incarcerated regularly commit suicide as a result. The dehumanizing treatment experienced by the Gerasene – which, we should note, is in Western countries disproportionately inflicted upon men of colour – has been described by the United Nations and Amnesty International as torture.

What all of this means, I suggest, is that in the case of the Gerasene, the treatment was at least as bad as the cure. This is not to suggest that prisoners today are possessed by demons – this rhetorical move would harmfully layer one form of social stigma with another – but rather to suggest that there is something we can learn from their stories. These horrifying experiences make it abundantly clear that solitary confinement and social ostracization would have harmed the Gerasene.

Moreover, it is possible that Luke might be hinting at the brutality of the man's treatment in the Gospel. In antiquity, as today, imprisonment was known to be psychically corrosive, personally destructive, and tortuous. In his *Toxaris* the second century CE writer Lucian describes an elite man named Antiphilus who is wrongly accused and imprisoned. Antiphilus 'became ill and was already in a bad way, as would be expected for a man sleeping on the ground and at night not even able to stretch out his legs because they are shackled in stocks' (*Tox.* 29). In Luke 8.26 the Gerasene begs Jesus not to torture him because Jesus had commanded the spirit to leave. But it is here, in this moment, and in response to the reference to torture, that we learn about the shackling. Perhaps, learning from experience, the man worries that Jesus too will bind him as regularly happens during exorcisms. Perhaps shackling is what he means by torture.

The story raises questions about the complicity of the whole community when one member is diagnosed with a demonic condition. If institutional structures can harm people by fragmenting their sense of self, and if unboundedness and fragmentation make one vulnerable to possession, then who bears responsibility for the man's condition?

Conclusion

What this brief study of Acts 16 and Luke 8 reveals is the sociality of demonic possession. We tend to imagine solitary individuals harbouring a secret about their spiritual status from the rest of the world. Yet, this was rarely the case. In both of the stories examined here there are others who manipulate, control and exploit those who are identified as possessed. In the case of the enslaved girl her spiritual status is unproblematic to others if they are able to financially profit from her supernatural abilities. In the case of the man with the Legion, whose status cannot be leveraged or monetized, he is stripped of his clothing, possessions, freedom and relationships. He is exiled from a community that can neither control nor commercialize him. Both sets of responses are motivated by the self-interest of others and come at great cost to the individuals concerned. And both sets of responses utilize the bloody realia of despotic institutions and technologies – shackles, chains, confinement, social alienation and enslavement – to reach their ends. These are not just narratives about cosmic evil, they are stories about social evils and communal failure.

When I attended the Vatican exorcism course in Rome, I asked what I thought was everyone's question, but in fact turned out to be just mine. It was this: Might a person, more specifically me, be possessed and not know it? I might, I was told, but one of the several hundred exorcists in the room would be able to tell. What is unclear, though, is whether on familial, communal and ecclesiastical levels we might be unaware of our complicity in possession. How do our actions, institutions, social structures, inequalities and expectations create environments for demonic activity to flourish? How does the distinction that we draw between demonic oppression, on one hand, and social and political oppression, on the other, empower those who are 'normal' to neglect and alienate some others? How do the identification, exploitation, treatment, and mistreatment of vulnerable and liminal members of our communities as possessed do violence to those people? And how might these responses not only exacerbate but also create the conditions, for what we call 'possession'? Such questions are not rhetorical, they should press upon our consciences and call us to action.

References

Jack Abbott, 1982, *In the Belly of the Beast: Letters from Prison*, New York: Vintage.

Luis Ménendez-Antuña, 2019, 'Of Social Death and Solitary Confinement: The Political Life of a Gerasene (Luke 8:26–39)', *Journal of Biblical Literature* 138.3, pp. 643–64.

Candida R. Moss, 2010, 'The Man with the Flow of Power: Porous Bodies in Mark 5.25–34', *Journal of Biblical Literature* 129.3, pp. 507–19.

Orlando Patterson, 2018, *Slavery and Social Death: A Comparative Study*, Cambridge: Harvard University Press.

Dan-el Padilla Peralta, 2017, 'Slave Religiosity in the Roman Middle Republic', Classical Antiquity 36.2, pp. 317–69.

Further reading

Katy E. Valentine, 2018, 'Reading the Slave Girl of Acts 16:16-18 in Light of Enslavement and Disability', *Biblical Interpretation* 26, pp. 352–68.

Contributors

Nicholas Adams is Professor of Philosophical Theology at the University of Birmingham.

Loveday Alexander is Professor Emerita of Biblical Studies in the University of Sheffield, and a former member of the Church of England's Faith and Order Commission.

Christopher C. H. Cook is Emeritus Professor of Spirituality, Theology and Health in the Institute for Medical Humanities at Durham University, and Honorary Chaplain at Tees, Esk & Wear Valleys NHS Foundation Trust.

Matthias Grebe is Lecturer in Theology and the Centre Lead at St Mellitus College in Chelmsford, Essex.

Isabelle Hamley is an Anglican priest, currently serving as Secretary for Theology and Theological Adviser to the House of Bishops in the Church of England. In 2024 she was appointed as Principal of Ridley Hall in Cambridge.

Nick Ladd is a retired Anglican priest who continues to work in missional accompaniment for congregations, spiritual accompaniment with clergy, and research on congregational formation.

Candida R. Moss is the Cadbury Professor of Theology at the University of Birmingham.

Hector M. Patmore is Associate Professor of Biblical Studies at the KU Leuven, Belgium, and an Anglican priest.

Anne Richards is a National Public Policy Adviser for the Church of England and convener of the ecumenical Mission Theology and Apologetics Group.

Jennifer Strawbridge is Associate Professor in New Testament Studies at the University of Oxford, G.B. Caird Fellow in Theology at Mansfield College, and Associate Priest at St Andrews Old Headington, Oxfordshire.

Index of Bible References

Index of Names and Subjects

Index of Names and Subjects

Printed in the USA
CPSIA information can be obtained
at www.ICGtesting.com
JSHW021335161124
73610JS00006B/39